CHILDREN AND YOUTH
Social Problems and Social Policy

CHILDREN AND YOUTH
Social Problems and Social Policy

Advisory Editor

ROBERT H. BREMNER

Editorial Board
Sanford N. Katz
Rachel B. Marks
William M. Schmidt

THE NATIONAL YOUTH ADMINISTRATION

PALMER O. JOHNSON and OSWALD L. HARVEY

ARNO PRESS
A New York Times Company
New York — 1974

HV
1431
.J6
1974

Reprint Edition 1974 by Arno Press Inc.

Reprinted from a copy in
The University of Illinois Library

CHILDREN AND YOUTH
Social Problems and Social Policy
ISBN for complete set: 0-405-05940-X
See last pages of this volume for titles.

Manufactured in the United States of America

Library of Congress Cataloging in Publication Data

Johnson, Palmer Oliver, 1891-
    The National Youth Administration.

    (Children and youth: social problems and social
policy)
    Reprint of the 1938 ed. published by the U. S. Government Printing Office, Washington, and issued as Staff study no. 13 of the U. S. Advisory Committee on Education.
    1. United States. National Youth Administration.
I. Harvey, Oswald L., joint author. II. Title.
III. Series. IV. Series: United States. Advisory
Committee on Education. Staff study no. 13.
HV1431.J6 1974   362.7'0973   74-1687
ISBN 0-405-05964-7

THE NATIONAL YOUTH ADMINISTRATION

by

PALMER O. JOHNSON and OSWALD L. HARVEY

with an introduction by

DOAK S. CAMPBELL

Staff Study Number 13

•

Prepared for

THE ADVISORY COMMITTEE ON EDUCATION

UNITED STATES
GOVERNMENT PRINTING OFFICE
WASHINGTON : 1938

THE ADVISORY COMMITTEE ON EDUCATION

Floyd W. Reeves, *Chairman*

W. Rowland Allen
Edmund deS. Brunner
Oscar L. Chapman
Elisabeth Christman
Gordon R. Clapp
Ernest G. Draper
Alice Edwards
Henry Esberg [1]
Mordecai Ezekiel
John P. Frey [2]
George L. Googe
Frank P. Graham

Luther Gulick
Rev. George Johnson
Charles H. Judd
Thomas Kennedy
Katharine F. Lenroot
Arthur B. Moehlman
Henry C. Taylor
T. J. Thomas
John H. Zink
George F. Zook
  Vice Chairman

Paul T. David, *Secretary*

---

[1] Deceased September 22, 1937.
[2] Resigned March 1, 1937.

FOREWORD BY THE COMMITTEE

The Advisory Committee on Education was appointed by the President of the United States on September 19, 1936, initially for the purpose of making a study of the experience under the existing program of Federal aid for vocational education, the relation of such training to general education and to prevailing economic and social conditions, and the extent of the need for an expanded program of Federal aid for vocational education. The Committee was requested to develop recommendations that would be available to the Congress and the Executive. Under its original assignment, the Committee was known as the President's Committee on Vocational Education.

In a later letter dated April 19, 1937, the President stated that he had been giving much thought to the general relationship of the Federal Government to education, that numerous bills in connection with educational matters were pending in the Congress, and that it was his understanding that the Committee was already in possession of much information bearing upon the subject. He therefore requested the Committee to give more extended consideration to the whole subject of Federal relationship to State and local conduct of education, and to prepare a report.

In accordance with this request, the Committee enlarged the scope of its work and prepared a comprehensive report, which was transmitted to the President on February 18, 1938, and was transmitted by him to the Congress on February 23, 1938. The report was printed as House Document No. 529, Seventy-fifth Congress, third session. An indexed edition of the report, differing in pagination but not in text, was also printed for public use by the Advisory Committee, and has been made widely available.[1]

---

[1] The Advisory Committee on Education, Report of the Committee, for sale by the Superintendent of Documents, U. S. Government Printing Office, Washington, D. C. Price 35 cents.

The Committee was assisted in its work by a temporary staff of specialists in education, public administration, and economics. The major function of this staff was to collect, analyze, and interpret available data bearing upon the problems under consideration by the Committee. Time did not permit any extensive amount of original research, and original research was not attempted except in areas where the existing information seemed entirely inadequate. The work of the staff did result, however, in a number of studies which present in convenient form a large amount of information bearing upon the status and problems of education in the United States.

The present volume is one of the studies prepared by the research staff. The statements and conclusions contained in it are those of the authors, and do not necessarily conform to those of the Committee. The findings of this study were considered by the Committee, however, in formulating the conclusions and recommendations that appear in its own report.

Dr. Palmer O. Johnson, the senior author of this study, is professor of education, University of Minnesota. Under the general supervision of Dr. Doak S. Campbell, dean of the Graduate School of Education and director of the Senior College, George Peabody College for Teachers, Dr. Johnson initiated the present study and devoted the summer of 1937 to field work, the collection of basic information, and the preparation of a preliminary report. After it became necessary for Dr. Johnson to return to the University of Minnesota, Dr. Oswald L. Harvey of the Committee's staff was assigned to work with Dr. Johnson in the completion of the study. Dr. Harvey brought together additional information and assisted in preparing the study for publication. The data included are in general those available at the end of 1937, although in some cases the study has been revised to include other data available up to May 1938, the time when the study was sent to press.

AUTHORS' ACKNOWLEDGMENTS

Special acknowledgments are due the officials of the National Youth Administration, who willingly cooperated in making available to the authors the materials in the national office and also assisted in collecting further information from State sources. Numerous other Federal, State, and private agencies and individuals also cooperated helpfully.

Dr. C. Currien Smith assisted in the general planning of the study. Mr. Joseph H. Daoust was of much assistance in the preparation of statistical and other data, and Miss Clare W. Butler compiled bibliographical material used by the authors.

CONTENTS

	Page
INTRODUCTION	IX
I. THE YOUTH PROBLEM	1
II. NATURE AND SCOPE OF THE NATIONAL YOUTH ADMINISTRATION	8
Organization	8
Administrative Personnel	12
The Youth Aided by the Programs	15
Expenditures	16
Concluding Statement	18
III. THE STUDENT AID PROGRAM	23
Nature and Scope of the Program	23
The Recipients of Student Aid	29
Higher Institutions Attended by Recipients of Student Aid	37
The College Aid Projects	38
Concluding Statement	42
IV. THE WORK PROJECTS PROGRAM	48
Nature and Scope of the Program	48
The Youth Employed	52
The Work Projects	61
Educational Provision for Youth on Work Projects	70
Concluding Statement	76
V. OTHER PROGRAMS	79
Vocational Guidance and Placement	79
Apprentice Training	82
Educational Camps for Unemployed Women	82
VI. EVALUATION OF THE CONTRIBUTIONS OF THE NATIONAL YOUTH ADMINISTRATION	86
The Relief Problem	86
Educational Concepts and Policies	88
Urgent Problems of Youth	89
Benefits to Local Communities	90
Federal Administrative Policy	90
APPENDIX A, Executive Orders Nos. 7086 and 7164	92
APPENDIX B, Tables	95
APPENDIX C, Types of Cosponsor on Youth Work Projects	100
APPENDIX D, Types of Work Activity in Which Youth Engage on Work Projects	102
INDEX	105
RESEARCH STAFF AND CONSULTANTS OF THE COMMITTEE	119
PUBLICATIONS ON THE COMMITTEE	121

CONTENTS

LIST OF TABLES

	Page
1. Number of Youth Participating in Major Programs, by Type of Program and by Month, September 1935 to November 1937	16
2. Number of Institutions Participating and Number of Students Aided, by Type of Program and by Month, September 1935 to November 1937	30
3. Distribution of School Aid Quota Allotments to Counties, by Size of Incorporated Places, 1936–37	33
4. Characteristics of Youth Recipients of Student Aid, December 1937	34
5. Institutions Participating in the College Aid Program, by Type of Institution, Student Quota, and Monthly Fund Allocation, 1936–37	38
6. Percentage Distribution of 7,083 College Aid Recipients in 388 Colleges, by Type of Work Activity, April 1937	39
7. Youth Employed on Work Projects, by Relief Status, Sex, and Month, January 1936 to November 1937	52
8. Previous Work Experience of 19,808 Work Project Youth Prior to National Youth Administration Employment, by Type of Work and Sex	56
9. Number of Youth Leaving National Youth Administration Work Projects, by Reason for Leaving, February to November, 1937	57
10. Duration of Employment of Relief Youth since First Assignment on Work Projects, by Wage Class, March 1937	59
11. Duration of Employment of Work Project Youth since First Assignment, by Type of Community, March 1937	60
12. Distribution of Youth Employed on Work Projects, by Type of Project, October 1937	62

LIST OF FIGURES

1. Organization Chart, National Youth Administration	10

INTRODUCTION

This study of the work of the National Youth Administration is limited to a description of its organization and programs, with some evaluation of its accomplishments. Recommendations arising from the study were submitted to the Advisory Committee on Education in memorandum form, and were considered by it in the preparation of its report to the President.

In carrying on this study, the authors were faced initially with the problem of securing adequate factual evidence. Monthly statistical reports concerning some phases of the programs were currently available. The files of the National Youth Administration contained a substantial amount of usable information in the form of special reports and studies by State directors of the National Youth Administration. Some information was available on a Nation-wide basis as the result of specific inquiries which have been made from time to time by the National Youth Administration.

These sources of information were all used and additional information was obtained, so far as feasible within the time limitations, through field trips, interviews, and questionnaires.

No doubt the study would have been greatly facilitated if more comprehensive records had been available at the central office of the National Youth Administration. Especially pertinent would have been complete records of the qualifications of the administrative and supervisory personnel, and a larger amount of reliable data concerning the social, educational, and employment characteristics of the youth receiving assistance through the various programs of the National Youth Administration.

Although it has not been possible to obtain and present all of the data that would be desirable for a comprehensive treatment of the work of the National Youth Administration, it is my opinion that an adequate sampling has been made for the purposes of this study. The study appears to be of sufficient validity to reflect correctly the status of the National Youth Administration and to give a somewhat general appraisal of its program.

DOAK S. CAMPBELL.

CHAPTER I

THE YOUTH PROBLEM [1]

Only during recent years has the status of youth emerged in the United States as a major social problem. While the population was growing and spreading over the continent, there was plenty of room for young people in search of experience and a place in economic society. The vast majority of the people were engaged in comparatively simple rural enterprises, and educational needs were few and rudimentary. Not until the latter part of the past century were public educational facilities made available on an extensive scale. Occupational specialization and high-pressure production are of relatively recent development. The census of 1920 was the first to reveal an excess of urban over rural population.

The intensely rapid growth of population, the full impingement of industrial expansion and organization on economic and social life, and the final limitation of the frontier together have operated to force the American people into a recognition of population problems as a whole. As might be expected, various groups in the population have been faced with problems peculiar to themselves. Children were menaced with the oppressive conditions of child labor; poorly educated peasant immigrants suffered from industrial exploitation; and old people were faced with dismissal, abandonment, and economic insecurity. The problems of chief concern to youth, as one of these major groups, related primarily to education and employment. Job specialization demanded a more deliberate and specific form of vocational training; intelligent participation in civic affairs called for a more extensive and prolonged period of general education;

---

[1] Unless otherwise indicated the term "youth" is used throughout this report to signify that group of persons who have completed their sixteenth birthday anniversary but have not yet arrived at their twenty-fifth birthday anniversary. The age limits thus specified are referred to in the text variously as "16-24", "16 to 24," and "16 to 24 inclusive", all of which phrases have the same meaning. Groups of narrower age limits within those here indicated are also referred to as youth, but in such instances the age limits are usually given.

and the complexity of social participation necessitated a period of conscious orientation and guidance which might serve to adjust the individual to the conditions and demands of the group as a whole.

The recent major economic depression precipitated these problems of population adjustment. Defects in the social organization became glaringly evident and the need for concerted action became imperative. The Federal Government provided the essential lead and initiated the emergency program. By virtue of necessity relief was the primary motive. But relief alone, it soon became obvious, could not provide an adequate solution. So far as possible the relief program had to be tempered with constructive planning which might help to resolve the fundamental problems of social and individual maladjustment and yield results of permanent social value. Plans of varying nature and effectiveness were introduced to meet the needs of the groups principally affected, and the National Youth Administration was set up as an integral part of the program.

Approximately one-sixth of the population of the United States falls within the age limits 16 to 24.[2] With the declining birth rate this proportion may be expected to diminish correspondingly, until such time as population structure and size may have become fairly stable. In 1870 there were two persons over 25 to every youth between the ages of 15 and 25; by 1930 this ratio had risen to 3 to 1; and it is estimated that by 1960 it will be as high as 4 to 1.[3] Thus youth would seem to become progressively less significant as a group for national consideration. Because youth constitute, however, the immediate group to assume active participation in political, social, and economic life, their preparation is vitally important to society as a whole. From this point of view they warrant the most concentrated attention.

Partly as an outcome of the population changes referred to above, youth fall heir to two especially significant social tendencies, one of which is to their advantage, the other not. As the proportion of young dependents in the population

---

[2] U. S. Bureau of the Census, Fifteenth Census of the United States: 1930, Population, vol. II, ch. 10, Age Distribution, table 7, p. 576, and table 20, p. 593.

[3] National Resources Committee, Population Statistics, I, National Data (Washington: 1937), table 3, p. 19.

grows smaller and the proportion of wage-earning adults larger, it becomes possible to devote more and more attention to the needs of the youth group. Because of the need for an informed and educated citizenry, youth are being encouraged and will continue to be encouraged to attend school, and to progress so far as their abilities will permit; educational facilities are being extended and improved; and the total educational offering is becoming more diversified to provide for specific individual needs.

By contrast with the increased educational opportunities thus made available, however, vocational opportunities for youth may be expected to diminish. Technological improvements tend to increase the number of units of production per man, but they also give rise to constant shifting of occupations and corresponding periods of unemployment and readjustment for large groups of workers. They increase the amount of leisure time permitted to the individual, but they also demand a narrower and more specific type of skill and preparation on the part of the worker. Increasing competition for available jobs is an inevitable concomitant of technological improvement and a rapidly aging population. In the future job preference will probably be given to those with experience. This tendency is already evident. Job opportunities for youth may be expected in time to become more and more circumscribed. Youth may have to remain in school longer because of lack of economic opportunity and the preference for somewhat older and more experienced workers.

The significance of these coming events, however, has not yet been fully appreciated. Many youth have already left school, but only a few have been accommodated in industry. It is estimated that about two-thirds as many youth are out of school and seeking work as are in school or college.[4]

Almost four-tenths (37.1 percent) of all new applicants at public employment offices during the period July 1936

---

[4] Enrollments in grade 11 through college, 1936-37, are estimated by the U. S. Office of Education at approximately 3,750,000; and from data supplied by the Census of Partial Employment, Unemployment and Occupations of November 1937 the authors have estimated that approximately 2,400,000 persons 16 to 24 years of age are either totally unemployed or engaged in emergency work. In arriving at this figure the authors have estimated the number of those registered in the census who were within the specific age group but have not attempted to adjust for those who did not register in the census.

through March 1937 were aged 16 to 24, but only three-tenths (26.9 percent) of all persons placed in jobs fell within those age limits.[5]

Many youth are out of school for several years—2, 3, even 5—before they obtain their first full-time job. The majority lack either vocational experience or vocational training, and even the young people who are employed are not adequately provided for. Those with specific training frequently find themselves unable to secure jobs for which they have been trained. Many have to accept blind-alley jobs; others are doing work which has little or no relationship either to aptitude or to training. Most of the jobs available are of the unskilled or semiskilled variety. Wages, too, are low, ranging from a bare subsistence level to about $20 a week, and the conditions and hours of work are frequently unsuitable. These unfortunate conditions are not, of course, all attributable to the depression but there can be no question that they have been considerably aggravated since 1929.

Few young people have received adequate vocational orientation. Thousands leave school not only without formal occupational preparation, but also without a plan. They have nothing to do, and they do not know what they are able to do. Without guidance the individual youth tends to select for himself occupations somewhat remote from his particular aptitudes or general level of ability, and so to lose valuable time or else to become a misfit. Industry is not prepared to spend time and money in giving the necessary orientation; and the schools from which the youth have come either are not interested in developing guidance programs, or, because of lack of public support and sufficient funds, have not been able to establish them.

Some of the unemployed youth would like to return to school or to continue with the studies which by necessity they may be forced to terminate. But either the school program has nothing more to offer that interests them, or the costs of further schooling are prohibitive. Although the facil-

---

[5] U. S. Department of Labor, Division of Standards and Research, Survey of Employment Service Information: Analysis of the Characteristics of More Than 5,000,000 Applicants in the Active File Inventory, April 1, 1937, and of New Applications and Placements During the Period from July 1, 1936 to March 31, 1937 (Washington: U. S. Government Printing Office, 1937), pp. 172-3.

ities for free education have been provided, the costs of maintenance are such that many youth cannot afford to avail themselves of these facilities. It has been the common experience of social workers and school principals that children who drop out of school come most frequently from families in the lower income brackets; and it is the general impression that the representation of students in college is directly related to the income of their families. Various ways of providing for needy youth, such as low tuition fees, scholarships, and the cooperative plan of alternative periods of study and gainful employment, were in fairly common practice at the college level even before the depression; and the inadequacy of these provisions was recognized. That similar need existed and still exists among high school students was not fully appreciated until the depression made it obvious.

Thus, despite the educational opportunities already available, there are still many youth who, for want of a modicum of assistance, cannot utilize them. For this condition of affairs the schools are not wholly to blame. To the extent that their programs of study are insufficiently diversified and adapted to the individual needs of students, the fault is undoubtedly theirs. They are taking steps to remedy the defect, but progress, especially at the higher levels, is slow. Meeting the educational needs of youth who lack the necessary economic resources to attend school, however, is the function of the people themselves. It is not sufficient to establish compulsory attendance laws unless adequate school facilities are provided, or to offer free schooling for all unless added provisions, especially in terms of maintenance, are furnished to make attendance possible.

By raising the upper level of compulsory attendance to age 18, providing the necessary resources for tuition and maintenance, and adapting the educational offering to the needs of youth, a large number of young persons now out of school and unemployed could be removed from the labor market and rehabilitated. Given guidance and appropriate training, the difficulties and stresses of their subsequent period of adjustment to employment conditions could be considerably reduced. Their problem is neither purely educational nor purely occupational, but a synthesis of both; it is essentially one of rehabilitation.

Unemployed youth out of school are caught between the upper and the lower millstones of necessity. On the one hand, without training or experience they are of little or no value to an employer; current laws relating to accident liability and insurance influence employers to give preference, if any, to the older youth; and the demand for higher educational qualifications has grown more and more insistent. On the other hand, without resources to prolong their schooling, or without confidence in the programs offered by the schools, these unemployed youth cannot prosecute that period of further preparation conducive to adequate participation in gainful employment. As a result, unless they are given direct encouragement and considerable rehabilitation, they almost inevitably constitute a focus of social maladjustment. Upon them is the curse of not being wanted, with all its concomitants of apathy or resentment and of personality disintegration. The possibilities of their engaging in anti-social behavior under such circumstances are obvious.

The Federal Government intervened to help remedy the plight of unemployed youth by the establishment successively of the Civilian Conservation Corps and the National Youth Administration. Although relief was inevitably one of the purposes in their establishment, the stimulation of educational interests and the economic and social rehabilitation of youth were also regarded as major objectives of these agencies. Turning the talents of youth to constructive ends, they sought to employ them on projects of economic value as well as of educational significance. The record of achievement of these agencies is considerable.

The youth program as a Federal emergency function began with the establishment of the Civilian Conservation Corps in April 1933. Later in the same year, at the University of Minnesota, a program of student aid at the college level was begun, supported by funds provided from the Federal Emergency Relief Administration. In February 1934 this form of aid, still under the control of the Federal Emergency Relief Administration, was extended throughout the country,[6] and involved, prior to the establishment of the Works Progress Administration, a total expenditure of approximately $15,000,000.[7] In May 1934 a program of resident camps and schools for unemployed women was established under the Federal Emergency Relief Administration;[8] eventually they became part of the National Youth Administration. One year later, on June 26, 1935, President Roosevelt by Executive order established the National Youth Administration as an autonomous division of the Works Progress Administration.[9]

The major objectives of the National Youth Administration are as follows:

> 1. To provide funds for the part-time employment of needy school, college, and graduate students 16 to 24 years of age so as to enable them to continue their education; and
> 2. To provide funds for the part-time employment of youth from relief families on work projects designed not only to give the young people valuable work experience, but also to benefit the communities in which they live.

Of these two programs, the former is usually referred to as the student aid program and the latter as the work projects program. Each will receive detailed consideration in the ensuing chapters of this study. In a separate chapter some brief mention will be made of other programs, relatively minor from the point of view of cost, which at one time or another have also been included in the total program of the National Youth Administration, namely, the junior guidance and placement service, the apprentice-training program, and the program of educational camps for unemployed women.

---

[6] FERA Communication E-15, February 2, 1934.
[7] Information supplied by the Division of Education Projects of the WPA. The exact amount was $14,875,550.
[8] FERA Communication E-24, May 23, 1934.
[9] Executive Order No. 7086, June 26, 1935. For text, as revised, see appendix A, which also contains the text, as revised, of Executive Order No. 7164, Prescribing Rules and Regulations Relating to Student-Aid Projects and to Employment of Youth on Other Projects under the Emergency Relief Appropriation Act of 1935. Other Executive orders relating to the NYA are No. 7123, August 1, 1935, listing the names of persons appointed as members of the National Advisory Committee and providing for their expenses per diem, and No. 7384, June 8, 1936, appointing two additional members to the National Advisory Committee.

CHAPTER II

NATURE AND SCOPE OF THE NATIONAL YOUTH ADMINISTRATION

In order to gain an adequate understanding of the various programs of the National Youth Administration it is necessary to know something of the general organization and administration of the agency. In this chapter are described the organization and administrative personnel of the Youth Administration, as well as the number of youth profiting from the program and the expenditures necessary to carry it out.

Organization

In accordance with the Executive order of June 26, 1935,[1] the National Youth Administration was set up as an agency within the Works Progress Administration. It is thus primarily a relief agency. It uses the available facilities of the Works Progress Administration in carrying out its program, but administratively the two agencies are separate. The research and statistical services of the Works Progress Administration are available to the National Youth Administration; youth eligible for employment on work projects are certified by the Works Progress Administration; the selection and assignment of youth are effected in accordance with the regular Works Progress Administration procedures;[2] the youth working on National Youth Administration projects are subject to Works Progress Administration safety regulations; and accidents occurring on National Youth Administration projects, and the compensation claims resulting therefrom, are handled by the Works Progress Administration.

The funds with which the National Youth Administration operates are earmarked from the general appropriation by

---

[1] Executive Order No. 7086, June 26, 1935. For text, see appendix A.
[2] In the student aid program the selection and certifying of recipients is in the hands of the school and college officials.

Congress for emergency relief. These funds are apportioned by the President to the two chief programs of the National Youth Administration, student aid and work projects. Within the limitations of the President's allotments the Youth Administration is free to divide the funds among the several States; distribution is effected in accordance with certain specifications based on the size of the youth relief population or, in the case of the college student aid program, on college enrollments.[3] National Youth Administration pay rolls and requisitions for equipment and supplies are handled through the appropriate divisions of the Works Progress Administration and of the United States Treasury.

Within the limitations specified above, the National Youth Administration has its own administrative organization, Federal, State, and local, which determines policies and procedures in the administration and supervision of its program throughout the Nation.

The national office consists of an executive director, who is also deputy administrator of the Works Progress Administration; a deputy executive director; an executive committee of 6 members from various Federal agencies; and a national advisory committee of 35 members, representative of labor, business, agriculture, education, and youth. An outline of the administrative organization of the National Youth Administration, which indicates national, regional, and State personnel and staff relationships, is presented in figure 1.[4]

The detailed operation of the National Youth Administration program in the several States varies according to local needs and problems. Youth administrations have been established in every State, in the District of Columbia, and in New York City. The program for each of these areas is administered by a State director and his staff. As a part of the State administrative organization, State advisory committees appointed by the national executive director have been set up to advise as to the most desirable type of youth

---
[3] Other specific limitations with regard to the eligibility of youth, the proportionate amount of funds to be expended for such items as wages, etc., are given in the more detailed description of each of the major programs of the National Youth Administration provided in later chapters of the study. It should be noted that this discussion is as of the time of writing, during the fiscal year ending June 30, 1938.

[4] Supplied by the NYA.

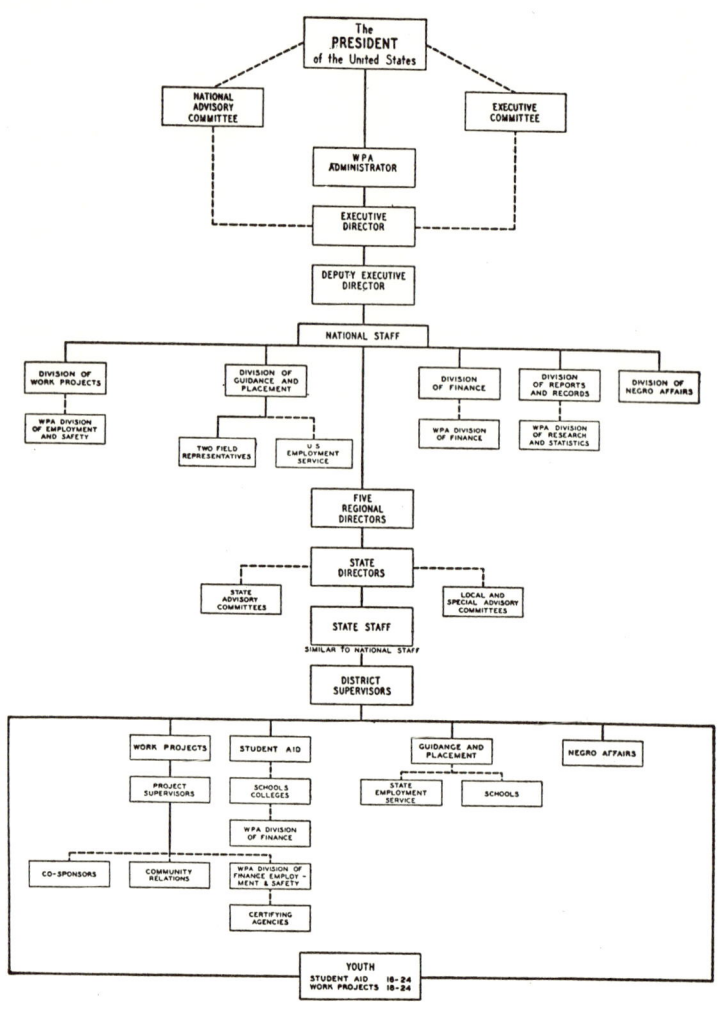

FIGURE 1.— Organization chart, National Youth Administration.

program for the State, to offer proposals for the development and the execution of the program, and to promote interest in it. Individual members frequently cooperate in planning work projects for youth and in fostering the development of State-wide projects.

As the local representative of the national executive director the State director sets up the machinery for the administration of the National Youth Administration program in his State, interprets the policies of the national office to his staff, and adapts general regulations to suit local conditions. With the approval of the national office he appoints his State and district personnel. Apart from the exceptions noted later, he gives final approval to all Youth Administration work projects in his State. Within certain limitations imposed by the national office he is permitted flexibility in the adaptation of these projects to State or local needs. He is required to cooperate with local officials of the Works Progress Administration in improving the effectiveness of the Youth Administration program.

The State director is advised and assisted by various division heads or supervisors, usually one for each of the main divisions of the program, who are functionally analogous to the directors of the corresponding divisions in the national office. For example, there is usually a head for the division of guidance and placement and one for the division of work projects. Within broad general requirements, however, the major part of the administration of the student aid program is usually placed in the hands of the State and college officials concerned.

For convenience and efficiency in administration, every State is divided into districts, each usually comprising several counties. For every district there is a supervisor responsible directly to the State director. Responsible to the district supervisor are the project supervisors, who provide the direct contact between the Youth Administration and the youth participating in its projects.

Local advisory committees constitute an integral part of the administrative organization of the National Youth Administration. Organized variously on a district, county, rural, urban, or other community basis, they assist the local officials of the Youth Administration by sponsoring projects, obtaining contributions, planning projects, interpreting the needs of youth, and promoting the National Youth Administration program generally.

To enlist and ensure the cooperation of the public in the execution and development of its program, the National Youth Administration has in principle worked in close cooperation with local, State, and other Federal governmental agencies and with numerous nongovernmental organizations. Relationships with these various agencies and groups are usually cordial, although there is some reason for thinking that occasionally cooperation is not sufficient for the most effective results.

Administrative Personnel

In evaluating the contributions of the National Youth Administration it is significant to know what the background, training, and experience have been of those individuals who are responsible for the formulation of its policies and for the planning and execution of its programs. Though the available information is incomplete, the following analysis provides a fairly comprehensive general summary of the characteristics of the administrative and supervisory staff.

The composition of the national administrative office and some of the essential characteristics of its personnel as of January 1938 may be summarized briefly as follows: The total of 23 persons is made up of the deputy executive director, 5 regional directors, 5 directors of administrative divisions, and 12 assistants. All 5 regional directors, 2 directors of divisions, and 7 assistants are men. Three staff members have Ph. D. degrees, 4 have master's degrees, 12 have bachelor's degrees or the equivalent, and 4 have less than a bachelor's degree. Two are Negroes. The vocational activities and interests of the group are principally educational; but sociology, law, accounting, architecture, journalism, and business and labor administration are also reported.[5]

---
[5] Data supplied by the NYA.

There are 50 State youth directors, ranging in age from 25 to 60, with a median age of about 41 years. Seven of the State directors are women. The majority of full-time salaries fall within the limits $3,600 to $4,800. In education the group ranges from persons with some college work without degree to those with the Ph. D. or its equivalent. The majority have bachelor's or master's degrees. Members of the group have held numerous kinds of administrative positions or public office; they have been engaged in many kinds of educational occupation, as well as a considerable number of other types of occupation; and they claim memberships in 24 different associations. Altogether, the State directors constitute a group of practical, versatile, socially competent, and fairly well-educated persons.[6]

The personnel records of 111 administrative and supervisory personnel, other than directors, attached to the State offices as of the summer of 1937, indicate that almost three-fourths are men and that about one-sixth are Negro. Ages range from 22 to 57, with the median slightly above 30. Annual salaries range from $1,000 to $3,600, with the median about $2,300. The Negroes in this group receive salaries definitely lower than those paid to the whites. Educational qualifications range from high school graduation to the Ph. D.; three-fourths of the group have a bachelor's degree or more. Previous work experience covers a wide variety of occupations, predominant among which are those in emergency Government agencies, the Y. M. C. A. and Y. W. C. A, the Boy Scouts and Girl Scouts, and schools and colleges. Education, social work, and civil service are the three major activities, experiences, and interests of this group.[7]

A sampling of 37 personnel records of State supervisors of work projects reveals as the typical supervisor a person about 35 years of age, receiving a salary of about $2,400 a year. A bachelor's degree is the average extent of academic qualification. The majority have had experience in educational work or in administration and supervision of various kinds.

---

[6] Data assembled during August 1937 by the staff of the Advisory Committee on Education from personnel files of the NYA. New York City and the District of Columbia have their own youth directors.

[7] Ibid.

A study of the personnel records of about 600 work project supervisors in 6 States [8] as of the summer of 1937 indicates that the typical individual work project supervisor is about as likely to be a man as a woman; is about 30 years of age; receives a monthly salary of from about $80 to $120, depending upon the State; has graduated from high school; and has had previous experience, most frequently in white-collar work.[9]

Personnel records of 32 State directors of student aid indicate that the median age of these officials is 32, and that their median salary is about $2,400. Two-thirds have a bachelor's degree or more; the remainder have had some college education. Work experience lies principally in the fields of education, journalism, and business.[10]

Thus, in general, the persons who administer the programs of the National Youth Administration may be characterized as follows: They are fairly well educated; they have had diversified work experience, though principally in the fields of education, social work, and public service; they are definitely older than the body of youth whom they serve, but are not much older; according to Government standards they are reasonably well paid; and they have a wide variety of interests.

Appointments to the staff of the Youth Administration are not made from civil service lists or through the procedures of any other type of formalized routine. Selection is based rather upon shrewd individual judgment, expediency, and considerable trial and error. Statistical information concerning turn-over is not available, but the general opinion is that although in the past it has been considerable, it is fairly certain that during the period subsequent to 1936 replacements have been relatively rare. Survival depends upon many different factors, among the most important of which are native intelligence; adaptability to local social, political, economic, and racial conditions; flexibility of ideas sufficient to facilitate adjustment to changing social concepts, a con-

---
[8] Ibid.
[9] The States included are California, Kansas, Kentucky, Nebraska, Louisiana, and Ohio.
[10] Ibid.

tinuously changing program, and urgently pressing new administration problems; and above all the enthusiasm that persists even in the face of the uncertainties resultant upon an annual budget for an emergency program.

In view of the unique character of the functions of the National Youth Administration, it is perhaps as well, at least during the experimental and formative stages of its existence, that the process of selecting personnel according to formalized procedures should not have been introduced A surprising outcome of these earlier years, considering the handicaps under which the program has operated, has been the really high quality of personnel employed. The relative success of the Youth Administration in this connection clearly shows that given a worth-while social objective, enthusiasm, and initiative, it is possible to develop effective workers out of material which might appear to be deficient in the attributes which a priori would seem to be the most desirable.

If and as a more stable period supervenes it should be possible to crystallize the valuable experience of the National Youth Administration in the personnel field and develop more formal appointment procedures. Experience, however, suggests that eventually it will be found to be true that the characteristics of successful workers in the field of youth problems are fundamentally different and distinct from those typical of educators on the one hand and of employment managers on the other.

The Youth Aided by the Programs

In table 1 are presented data concerning the number of youth (i. e., persons 16 to 24 years of age) participating in the major programs of the National Youth Administration.

The total number of youth receiving aid on the major programs rose from a median of about 470,000 a month during the first 6 months of 1936 to a median of more than 580,000 a month during the first 6 months of 1937. Since that time the total budget has been reduced; consequently the trend in the number of recipients, after allowance has been made for seasonal variation, has declined. During its peak month, April 1937, the National Youth Administration was aiding almost 630,000 youth on its 2 major programs alone, seven-tenths of them through the student aid program. For the entire period of the existence of the National Youth Administration, up to and including November 1937,[11] the median monthly number of recipients on the two programs combined has been about 406,000.

TABLE 1.—*Number of youth participating in major programs, by type of program and by month, September 1935 to November 1937* [1]

Year and month	Total	Number receiving student aid	Number employed on work projects
1935:			
September	34,924	34,924	
October	183,594	183,594	
November	234,450	234,450	
December	282,829	282,829	
1936:			
January	322,380	306,490	15,890
February	426,186	351,302	74,884
March	539,229	380,099	159,130
April	581,093	404,749	176,344
May	571,366	398,362	173,004
June	394,002	214,603	179,399
July	160,422	239	160,183
August	158,772	1,707	157,065
September	224,872	62,969	161,903
October	502,292	341,583	160,709
November	567,133	400,253	166,880
December	584,431	412,210	172,221
1937:			
January	597,400	418,721	178,679
February	611,315	428,818	182,497
March	626,661	442,100	184,561
April	628,713	443,986	184,727
May	602,702	425,694	177,008
June	415,233	249,826	165,407
July	143,707		143,707
August	127,366	35	127,331
September	157,588	35,673	121,915
October	362,046	243,862	118,184
November	405,671	283,269	122,402

[1] Summary of tables 2 and 7.

Expenditures

From funds provided through the several Federal Emergency Relief Appropriation Acts the National Youth Administration expended during the fiscal years 1935–37 a total of

[11] At the time of writing the latest available statistics referred to November 1937.

approximately $102,500,000;[12] for the current year, 1937-38, it has been allocated a further sum of approximately $50,000,000.[13]

Of the total of approximately $39,000,000 expended during the fiscal year 1935-36, three-fifths (approximately $24,000,000) went to student aid, and two-fifths (approximately $15,000,000) went to work projects. For the fiscal year 1936-37 the reverse distribution obtained. Of the total of approximately $63,500,000 expended, two-fifths (approximately $28,000,000) went to student aid, and three-fifths (approximately $35,500,000) went to work projects.[14] Out of the total of approximately $50,000,000 provided by the Emergency Relief Appropriation Act of 1937, two-fifths (approximately $19,000,000) goes to student aid, and three-fifths (approximately $31,000,000) to work projects.[15]

The administrative expenses of the National Youth Administration are included as part of those of the Works Progress Administration.[16] In the 2 years, 1935-37, they constituted a sum equal to slightly less than 5 percent of the total allotments provided for disbursement on the student aid and work projects programs. For the fiscal year 1935-36 they totaled approximately $2,000,000, of which 9 percent went to the national office and the remainder to the State offices. During 1936-37 they totaled almost $2,500,000, of which approximately 11 percent went to the national office. For the first 6 months of 1937-38 administrative expenses

---

[12] Report of the President of the United States to the Congress, Showing the Financial Status of Funds Provided in the Emergency Relief Appropriation Acts of 1935, 1936, and 1937, as of December 1937 (January 8, 1938), pp. 305-6.

[13] Presidential Letters No. 7048, July 8, 1937, and No. 7502, December 20, 1937.

[14] Report of the President * * * Showing the Financial Status of Funds Provided in the Emergency Relief Administration Appropriation Acts of 1935, 1936, and 1937 * * * loc. cit.

[15] Presidential Letters No. 7048 and No. 7502.

[16] They include the following items: Personal services (salaries); supplies and materials; communication service; travel expense; freight and express; printing and binding; heat, light, and power; rent of buildings; rent of equipment; miscellaneous items; guidance and placement program; apprentice training program; advertising and publication of notices.

Funds for the women's camps program under the NYA were provided for through a separate allocation. Presidential Letter No. 5064, July 13, 1936 (together with supplements), established a limitation of $1,166,000, of which, however, only $700,000 was actually allocated. The program operated as an official work project (OP. 165-9002), and closed October 1, 1937. Information supplied by the NYA.

amounted to approximately $1,250,000, only 9 percent of which went to the national office.[17]

The average annual Federal expenditure per relief youth employed on the work projects program for 1936–37 was approximately $225, and per youth receiving student aid approximately $72.[18] In interpreting these averages, however, the following factors should be kept in mind:

1. In the student aid program a considerable share of the burden of cost is borne by participating institutions, and in the work projects program some of the costs are borne by local cosponsors. Consequently, the size of the Federal contribution is probably less than it would be under a more centralized system.

2. The burden of cost borne by the National Youth Administration is still further reduced through the contribution of essential services, of considerable but indeterminable value, in the way of statistical reporting, certification, etc., by other Federal agencies, especially the Works Progress Administration. It should be remembered, however, that almost all governmental units, and especially those of an emergency nature, are dependent upon one another to some extent for administrative or technical assistance.

3. Because so little of the cost of administration is chargeable to the student aid program, and because the minor programs of the National Youth Administration involve relatively small expenditures, it has been found convenient, in determining the above averages, to charge all administrative overhead to the work projects program. Consequently the total administrative overhead and the total Federal contribution to work projects have been charged to the work projects program, and only the aid extended to students, school and college combined, has been charged to the student aid program.

---

[17] Data supplied by the NYA.
[18] Data supplied by the NYA. These average expenditures do not constitute the simple arithmetic average of the figures reported above.

Concluding Statement

The National Youth Administration is nominally a relief agency constituting an integral part of the Works Progress Administration. It is, however, administratively semiautonomous.

The functions of the National Youth Administration have been expressed in the form of five programs. The student aid program provides for those youth who otherwise are financially unable to continue their schooling. The work projects program provides work experience for those youth whose interest in further schooling is relatively weak, but who find it imperative to obtain work experience as a qualification for admission to private employment and at the same time to earn a living. The guidance and placement service provides orientation for youth concerning their occupational future and attempts to place them in employment. The apprentice-training program was only an incidental function of the National Youth Administration; recently it has been transferred to the Department of Labor. The program of educational camps for unemployed women was found to be expensive to maintain; for this and other reasons the program has been terminated.

The administrative organization of the National Youth Administration, both national and State, is simply conceived and effective. Relations of the Youth Administration with private agencies and with other Federal and State governmental agencies which have a direct interest in the affairs and welfare of youth are generally cordial and effective. The use of advisory committees at all administrative levels is an important administrative device which has undoubtedly been effective in promoting the welfare of youth.

Despite the fact that the available supply of competent personnel is limited, that appointments are only temporary, and that operations are restricted by an annual budget, it is probably not an exaggeration to conclude that, in terms of previous experience and adaptability, the administrative and supervisory personnel of the Youth Administration at all levels is comparable with current civil service standards.

The median number of youth receiving aid on the two major programs has been about 406,000 a month; at the peak the total approximated 630,000.

Overhead administrative costs are maintained at an unusually low level, primarily because of the policy of decentralized administration and because several of the essential services are provided by other Federal agencies, in particular the Works Progress Administration, and by cooperative arrangements with institutions and local bodies. Since the establishment of the National Youth Administration in June 1935, expenditures for all purposes have totaled approximately $102,500,000; and an additional sum of about $50,000,000 has been allotted for the year 1937-38. Average Federal expenditures per youth receiving aid on the two major programs for the year 1936-37 were approximately $72 for all types of student aid and approximately $225 for work projects.

In terms of expenditures and the numbers of youth aided, the National Youth Administration may be said to have performed a valuable service inexpensively. Administrative overhead constitutes a negligible fraction of the total expenditures, and expenditures per youth in receipt of aid are low by comparison with those on programs of similar function.

Any emergency governmental function may be expected to suffer from two major defects—excessive turn-over of personnel and unstable policies. That the National Youth Administration is open to criticism on both of these scores is true, but more significant is the fact that in both respects the deficiencies are relatively slight. Personnel replacements are now comparatively rare; most of the administrative staff that remains has been employed since near the beginning of the program. And although changes in policy have been inevitable, and have sometimes been made in apparently arbitrary fashion, it is the considered opinion of members of the staff of the national office that most changes have been introduced only after careful scrutiny and consideration of past experience, and after consultation with leading authorities in the fields of education, employment, and youth problems. In this connection, it is the opinion of the national director that the contribution of advisory bodies has proved of inestimable value.

The operating principle of the National Youth Administration is essentially democratic. It is possible that the Administration may profit further from this technique through its extension to include the youthful participants themselves.

Although its decisions must inevitably recognize, first, the relationship of the youth problem to the problems of the Nation as a whole, and, second, the fact that the National Youth Administration is in its present form fundamentally a relief agency, there can be no question that the Youth Administration itself is sympathetic with the fundamental needs and problems of youth. In actual operation the National Youth Administration has transcended the immediate problem of relief and has ventured, with considerable success, into educational and employment fields which might have been deemed entirely outside of its province. In so doing, it has demonstrated possibilities of profound social significance; and its very unusualness as an agency has made possible the novel and productive approach that has characterized its development from the beginning.

After several years of experimentation, the National Youth Administration is perhaps now at the stage of development in which some permanent long-time policy and a more stable form of administration would be justifiable. Should such changes be contemplated, the characteristics of the personnel could well be subject to scrutiny as a means both of eliminating the unsuitable and of determining what specifically are the attributes most appropriate for successful achievement in this unusual field of governmental activity.

The need for an administrative unit dealing specifically with the problems of out-of-school youth in terms of consistent and carefully planned policies of a permanent implication is most clearly urgent. It is desirable that as early as is conveniently possible the functions of the Youth Administration should be incorporated into the regular governmental structure. Whether the agency of administration should be Federal, or State, or both, is a topic not within the framework of reference of this study. In view of the experimental nature of the present program, it would seem well to continue it for a time on a basis of Federal administration, but with increased emphasis upon State cooperation. In any case, it is desirable that special care be taken to assure a well-qualified personnel of wide experience, adaptable personality, and adequate comprehension of both the educational and the employment problems of youth. After a few years of further experimentation, the program should be subject to review, and the basis of distribution of effective functions and administration between Federal and State authorities should then be carefully considered.

There might be some advantage in changing the name of the unit administering the youth program in such a way as to imply not the administration of youth but rather the provision of services to youth. For this reason it is suggested that the designation of the agency be changed to Youth Service Administration.

CHAPTER III

THE STUDENT AID PROGRAM

This chapter constitutes a consideration of student aid with reference to the nature and scope of the program, the recipients of aid, the types of institutions that these recipients attend, and the types of projects on which they are engaged.

Nature and Scope of the Program

Federal aid to enable qualified young men and women to attend college was first provided in 1934 under the direction of the Federal Emergency Relief Administration.[1] With the establishment of the student aid program of the National Youth Administration in 1935, the scope of this initial provision was extended both above and below the college level.[2] In the National Youth Administration program the recipients of student aid are divided into three classes: (1) Pupils in elementary and high schools; (2) undergraduate students in college; and (3) graduate students.[3] All divisions of the program require that the youth aided shall be from 16 to 24 years of age.[4]

The school aid program.[5]—That division of the student aid program in which the recipients are elementary and high-school pupils is designated the school aid program. All institutions participating in this program must be nonprofit making and tax exempt. They must be bona fide educational institutions, and certified as such by the chief State school officer. The head of any particular institution concerned submits to the State youth director an affidavit certifying that

---

[1] FERA Serial Communication E-15, February 2, 1934.
[2] See appendix A.
[3] The distinction between undergraduate aid and graduate aid is not always clearly marked.
[4] The stipulations governing the student aid program described here are those specified for 1937-38. In general the requirements are the same as those which have been in operation since the beginning of the program. Changes will be pointed out when significant.
[5] School Aid 1937-38, NYA Bulletin No. 9 (August 12, 1937), 9 pp. Mimeographed.

the institution is of elementary or of high school character; that the pupils to receive aid will be selected in accordance with the prescribed eligibility requirements; and that in the event of acceptance the institution will comply with all regulations of the National Youth Administration. Before approval by the State youth director, the affidavit must be endorsed by the public school superintendent of the city, county, or independent school district concerned and by the chief State school officer.

Certain requirements govern the eligibility of pupils to receive aid. In order to qualify on the basis of need for such assistance, an applicant for aid must produce satisfactory evidence, verified as to authenticity and sufficient to indicate that he could not enter or remain in school without employment on the student aid program; that he is a citizen of the United States or has filed declaration of intention to become a citizen; and that he is of good character and possesses such ability as to give assurance of performing good scholastic work. School aid is discontinued for pupils who fail to pass in at least three-fourths of their scholastic work. Only pupils who carry at least three-fourths of the normal school load may receive aid.

The determination of the eligibility of pupils for school aid is the responsibility of the officials of the institutions which they attend. Every pupil or prospective pupil desiring assistance under the program must make his application on an official form of such nature as to assist the responsible school officials in the determination of his need. Applications for school aid must be approved by the principal of the school and by the city or county superintendent of the school system concerned. In selecting the most needy applicants, school officials may make use of the facilities of available public or private agencies or may use individual references.

School aid employment quotas were originally set at 7 percent of the number of persons aged 16 to 24 reported to be on relief during May 1935, as determined by a census conducted by the Works Progress Administration.[6] The funds

---

[6] NYA Circular Y-6 (August 15, 1935), 4 pp. Mimeographed.

for school aid for 1937–38 are allocated to each State on the basis of approximately 75 percent of the funds used in 1936–37.[7] Without prior approval of the State youth director, no school is permitted to employ on school aid projects a number of pupils greater than 10 percent of its total regular enrollment on October 1, 1936. The ratio of youth in a racial minority group to the total youth aided on the program may be not less than the ratio which the minority group bears to the total population of the school district or State concerned.

The maximum amount that any pupil may earn is $6 per month. The hourly wage rates are based on the rates prevailing in the institution or locality for the same type of work. The maximum hours of work are 7 per day on nonschool days, 3 per day on school days, and 20 per week.

It is stipulated that the work performed by pupils receiving aid should be practical and useful. Emphasis is placed on work that is adapted to their abilities and major interests. Youth receiving aid may not be employed to displace workers paid from other funds.

Institutions wishing to participate in the student aid program are required to submit to the State youth director for approval a form describing the proposed institutional work plan.[8] The work to be performed must be classified and described under the following major categories: Clerical, construction, departmental service, library work, duplication, grounds and building maintenance, research and surveys, home economics, art, laboratory assistance, recreation, and miscellaneous.

The college and graduate aid program.[9]—The college and graduate aid program is designed for students in approved institutions that require high school graduation or the equivalent as a minimum for entrance. Aid given to undergraduate students or to professional students who have not obtained their bachelor's degree is known as college aid; aid given to students who have obtained their bachelor's degree and are pursuing graduate work is called graduate aid.

---

[7] Information supplied by the NYA.
[8] Prior to 1937–38 the submission of a proposed work plan for student aid was not mandatory.
[9] College and Graduate Aid 1937–38, NYA Bulletin No. 10 (August 12, 1937), 11 pp. Mimeographed.

As in the case of the school aid program, all institutions participating in the college and graduate aid program must be certified by the chief State school officer as nonprofit-making, tax-exempt, bona fide educational institutions. They must be of collegiate grade, and in the graduate aid program they must be of university character. Affidavits on an official form must be submitted by the head of each institution for endorsement by the chief State school officer and for approval by the State youth director. Included as part of this affidavit is a statement [10] setting forth the amount of assistance of all types extended to students by the institution during the previous year.

The requirements for eligibility of students are the same as those for school aid. The student must produce satisfactory evidence to show that he could not enter or remain in school without employment on the student aid program, that he is a citizen or has filed declaration of intention to become one, that he is of good character and possesses the ability to do or to continue to do good scholastic work, and that he is a resident student carrying at least three-fourths of the normal load. The officials of the participating institutions are responsible for determining the eligibility of the individual students to receive college or graduate aid, and, in validating their claims as to the extent of need, may make use of public and private agencies.

The National Youth Administration establishes the fund quota for each institution accepted as eligible.[11] The maximum quota for any institution participating in the 1937–38 program is based upon the total number of resident undergraduate and graduate students under 25 years of age enrolled in that institution on October 1, 1936, who were carrying at least three-fourths of a normal load. The monthly fund quota is a figure equal to 8 percent of this

---

[10] An innovation with the 1937-38 program.
[11] The quota for college aid for the years 1935–36 and 1936–37 was based upon 12 percent of the college enrollment as of October 1, 1934. For graduate aid there were two divisions: (1) The quota for first year graduate students was determined on the basis of 20 percent of the number of master's degrees awarded during the preceding year; (2) the quota for advanced graduate aid was determined on the basis of 75 percent of the number of doctor's degrees awarded during the preceding year. A slight degree of flexibility of administration in the allotment of quotas was allowed.

enrollment multiplied by $15. If the students aided receive on the average less than $15 per month, the number of students who may be aided may exceed 8 percent of this enrollment. But the total allotment may not exceed an average of $15 per student aided per month for a period of 9 months. The regulations permit some degree of flexibility in the distribution of funds throughout the year. The maximum amount payable to a student receiving college aid during any one month is $20; to a student receiving graduate aid it is $40.

The maximum hours of work for both college and graduate aid students are 8 per day and 30 per week. During vacation periods within the academic year, however, the weekly maximum is 40 hours. It is provided that the wage rates per hour shall be the same as those prevailing in the institution or locality for the same type of work.

The institution is in each case responsible for the assignment of students to suitable work projects and for the supervision of the work that is done. It is stipulated that the projects shall be practical and useful, and that emphasis shall be placed on work that fits the abilities and major interests of the student. The institution is required to submit a work plan on a special form [12] to the State youth director for approval, if possible simultaneously with the institution's affidavit, but not later than the date of filing of the initial time report of the institution for the school year. The work to be performed must be classified and described, as in the school aid program, under the 12 following major categories: Clerical, construction, departmental service, library work, duplication, grounds and building maintenance, research and surveys, home economics, art, laboratory assistance, recreation, and miscellaneous.

In addition to the graduate aid progam described above, there is a special Negro graduate aid program.[13] Eligible Negro graduate students who cannot be cared for within the quota for graduate aid of a particular institution, after it has made a just allocation for Negro graduates from its regular

---

[12] An innovation with the 1937-38 program.
[13] NYA Bulletin No. 10, sec. 7.

quota, may apply through the institution which they desire to attend for assistance from the special Negro graduate aid fund set aside by the National Youth Administration. This institution in turn may apply through the office of the State youth director to the Washington office of the National Youth Administration for an additional sum for Negro graduate aid.

Expenditures.—The sum expended on the student aid program during the fiscal year 1935–36 totaled approximately $24,000,000,[14] of which about 40 percent went to school aid, 56 percent to college aid, and 4 percent to graduate aid.[15] Average cost per student aided on the program as a whole was approximately $78 for the year.[16]

For the fiscal year 1936–37 expenditures totaled approximately $28,000,000,[17] of which about 41 percent went to school aid, 55 percent to college aid, and 4 percent to graduate aid.[18] Annual costs on the program as a whole were approximately $72 per student aided.[19]

A total of approximately $19,000,000 has been allotted for the fiscal year 1937–38.[20]

It should be recognized, however, that the National Youth Administration is not the only agency providing funds to needy students. At the college level particularly, a considerable amount of financial assistance to students is provided by the institutions themselves. According to affidavits submitted [21] to the National Youth Administration by the approved colleges participating in the college and graduate program, a total of almost $38,500,000 was contributed by these institutions during 1936–37 in the form of scholarships, fellowships, grants-in-aid, loans to students, and amounts expended on regular operations such as for student assistants. During the same period the National Youth Administration

---

[14] See p. 17.
[15] Estimates based on pay-roll figures giving actual amounts paid out as accounted for by voucher checks to date from the total sum allotted. Data supplied by the NYA.
[16] See discussion on p. 18.
[17] See p. 17.
[18] Data supplied by the NYA.
[19] See p. 18.
[20] See p. 17.
[21] As required by regulation. See NYA Bulletin No. 10. This item was included for the first time in 1937. Summary of statistics supplied by the NYA. See appendix B, table 1.

THE STUDENT AID PROGRAM 29

disbursed to students in receipt of student aid at the same institutions a total of almost $16,250,000. The institutions aided 331,775 students, the National Youth Administration aided 180,990.[22] Students aided by the institutions received an average of $116 each as against an average of $90 received by students aided by the National Youth Administration.[23]

In other words, although the institutions spent more than two and one-third times as much for aid in 1936–37 as did the National Youth Administration, they aided only about twice as many students, at an average grant per individual about one and one-third times as great as that provided by the National Youth Administration. Recipients aided by the Federal Government are required to work for their aid, whereas much of the aid provided by the institution does not call for this type of return.

The Recipients of Student Aid

The total number of recipients under the student aid program varies from month to month, depending upon the activities of educational institutions (table 2). The summer months reflect the lowest totals; the maximums occur during the early spring months. Seldom is there a month in which no students are aided, because a few youth, particularly those on the school aid program, remain on the pay rolls of some institutions even during the summer months.

If the months of July, August, and September are excluded from consideration, the median enrollment during the academic year 1935–36 for all types of aid combined was 306,490; for the year 1936–37 it was 418,721. The corresponding medians for the various programs were, for school aid 189,031 and 276,584; for college aid 117,287 and 137,250; and for graduate aid 5,218 and 5,416. Thus the

---

[22] It should be noted that duplication occurs here, in that a student may receive aid from both sources. It should also be noted that the total here reported exceeds any monthly total reported in table 2 because the latter represents the total number of students receiving aid during each month, whereas the former represents the total number of different persons receiving aid during the year.

[23] The per capita average of $90 here reported represents the earnings of only college and graduate students. The $72 per capita reported on p. 28 represents average earnings of students on high-school and college- and graduate-aid programs combined. The $90 average is not altogether reliable even as a measure of college and graduate aid since it is not based on an unduplicated count of students aided.

greatest proportionate increase has occurred in the school aid program and the least in the graduate aid program. Recipients of school aid have constituted almost two-thirds of all participants in the student aid program in each year.

TABLE 2.—*Number of institutions participating and number of students aided, by type of program and by month, September 1935 to November 1937* [1]

Year and month	Number of institutions participating	Number of students aided			
		Total	School pupils	College students	Graduate students
1935:					
September	4,159	34,924	26,163	8,700	61
October	10,689	183,594	75,033	104,969	3,592
November	14,955	234,450	118,273	111,500	4,677
December	17,236	282,829	159,158	118,453	5,218
1936:					
January	18,403	306,490	189,031	112,654	4,805
February	19,613	351,302	227,629	118,623	5,050
March	20,076	380,099	256,706	117,287	6,106
April	19,831	404,749	275,544	122,498	6,707
May	18,474	398,362	266,304	125,758	6,300
June	6,932	214,603	127,121	80,932	6,550
July	39	239	239		
August	163	1,707	1,707		
September	4,875	62,969	52,155	10,730	84
October	19,906	341,583	207,954	128,771	4,858
November	23,247	400,253	257,475	137,250	5,528
December	23,794	412,210	270,464	136,572	5,174
1937:					
January	24,458	418,721	276,584	136,733	5,404
February	24,743	428,818	283,738	139,541	5,539
March	24,948	442,100	294,456	142,127	5,517
April	24,658	443,986	297,871	140,699	5,416
May	22,672	425,694	280,427	139,841	5,426
June	10,555	249,826	153,168	92,382	4,276
July					
August	12	35	35		
September	4,331	35,673	30,863	4,675	135
October	19,398	243,862	155,041	86,797	2,024
November	22,318	283,269	188,332	92,648	2,289

[1] Employment, Hours and Earnings of Students Assisted on the Student Aid Program of the National Youth Administration * * * September 1935 through November 1937, Works Progress Administration, Division of Research, Statistics, and Records; Student Aid Series R-1194 (January 18, 1938), tables 7-10.

April 1937, the month with the largest enrollment to date, provides an excellent cross-section picture of the student aid program in operation. Of the students aided during that month 67 percent were receiving high school aid, 32 percent were receiving undergraduate college aid, and 1 percent were receiving graduate aid.[24] It is interesting

[24] Employment, Hours and Earnings of Students Assisted on Student Aid Programs of the National Youth Administration, * * * Month Ending April 30, 1937, Works Progress Administration, Division of Research, Statistics and Records; Student Aid Series (May 27, 1937), tables 7-10.

to compare this distribution with that of all students in grades at these levels; the figures for all students above the elementary level for 1935–36 indicate 84 percent at the secondary level, 15 percent at the undergraduate college level, and 1 percent at the graduate level.[25] Evidently the student aid program is particularly emphasized at the undergraduate college level, and so operates to increase enrollments in higher institutions. At the graduate level male students are represented (76 percent)[26] on the aid program proportionately more heavily than they are (60 percent)[27] for graduate students as a whole. This difference does not obtain at the undergraduate level.

It should, however, be noted, first, that the bias reported in the above two paragraphs reflects a selective process inherent not only in the quota system of the National Youth Administration but also in the admission requirements of the institutions concerned; and, second, that apparently the general effect of the selective process is to make use of student aid provisions to compensate for deficiencies already present in the educational system at large.

The wage received for work done in return for student aid varies according to the type of institution. During the month of April 1937 the average earnings per high school student totalled $4.89; per college undergraduate student, $12.65; and per graduate student, $23.32. Average earnings vary slightly from month to month, but these figures are fairly representative of the amounts received.

Because Federal funds for the student aid program are limited in amount, and because the quota regulations restrict the amount of funds that any institution may utilize on the student aid program, the students actually aided are selected from a much larger group of applicants. Although comprehensive statistics in this connection are not available, certain data relating to conditions for 1936–37 will serve to demonstrate this difference between number of

---

[25] Data supplied by the U. S. Office of Education.
[26] See p. 30, footnote 24.
[27] Data supplied by U. S. Office of Education.

applicants and persons aided.[28] Out of a reported total of 371,673 persons who applied for school aid, the maximum aided during any month (297,871) constituted four-fifths of the total. Similarly, for college aid out of 216,546 requests, two-thirds (142,127) were aided; and for graduate aid out of 6,942 applicants, four-fifths (5,539) were aided. Thus, considered as a grand total, three-fourths of the applicants received student aid.

The effect of this selective process, which, within the limits of the allotted quotas, is the function of the educational institution concerned and not of the National Youth Administration, is reflected, at least as part of the total picture, in the available records of scholastic achievement of student aid recipients.[29] From reports received from a very limited number of high schools (397 out of a total of 22,880 institutions) there would appear to be no clearly marked difference in scholastic achievement between pupils receiving and those not receiving aid: 169 schools rated the pupils in receipt of aid higher than other pupils, 139 rated them lower, and 89 reported no essential difference. At the college level, on the other hand, the evidence in favor of students receiving aid is more conclusive. Reports were obtained from 270 out of 1,670 institutions: 168 rated the college aid students higher than other students in academic achievement, 71 rated them lower, and 31 indicated no essential difference. On the basis of this evidence it may be inferred that recipients of student aid are in general at least equal if not indeed superior to other students in scholastic achievement.

The distribution of school aid quotas among the youth in communities of various sizes corresponds to some extent with the distribution of youth in the total population in such communities. This is shown in table 3, in which the counties of residence are classified according to the incorporated community with the largest population within their confines. In general the more rural counties, presumably with youth

---

[28] Data compiled by the NYA from replies to NYA Circular Y-40 (November 25, 1936), 2 pp. Mimeographed. See appendix B, table 2, and discussion of quota provisions, pp. 26-27.

[29] Data compiled by the NYA from replies to NYA Circular Y-46 (February 26, 1937), 1 p. Mimeographed. See also, p. 30, table 2, footnote 1. No reports were requested from 193 graduate schools.

constituting larger proportions of their total populations, are receiving the larger share of the school aid quota.

TABLE 3.—*Distribution of school aid quota allotments to counties, by size of incorporated places, 1936–37* [1]

Counties with—	Percentage distribution of total United States population, 1930	Distribution of school-aid quota, 1936–37	
		Number	Percent
All counties	100.0	242,771	100.0
No incorporated places over 2,500	12.9	44,762	18.4
Incorporated places 2,500 to 9,999	19.6	56,193	23.2
Incorporated places 10,000 to 24,999	10.7	32,342	13.3
Incorporated places 25,000 and over	56.8	109,474	45.1

[1] Data compiled by the NYA from replies to NYA Circular Y-40 (Nov. 25, 1936), 2 pp. Mimeographed.

The provision that the recipient of college or graduate aid need not attend an institution in the State of his residence has permitted considerable mobility of college aid students. Out of every 20 college aid students, 3 are attending college in a State other than that of their legal residence.[30] More than one-half (56.6 percent) of those who migrate to other States, however, still remain in States within the same general region.[31] In other words, the migration, generally speaking, is not to remote States but rather to those near at hand.

States are not required to submit separate statistics relating to the racial distribution of recipients of student aid, but a number of them do so report. Consequently some evidence in this connection is available. In November 1937 in 12 Southern States [32] and the District of Columbia, having a large percentage of Negroes in the population, one-fourth (23.4 percent) of all pupils receiving school aid and about one-eighth (14.0 percent) of college and graduate aid recipients were Negroes. The significance of these figures may be

---

[30] Data supplied by the NYA. Both graduate and undergraduate students are included. See appendix B, table 3.
[31] Data supplied by the NYA. See appendix B, table 4.
[32] Alabama, Arkansas, Florida, Georgia, Kentucky, Mississippi, Missouri, North Carolina, South Carolina, Tennessee, Texas, and Virginia. Data supplied by the NYA.

appreciated by comparison with census data [33] relating to the percentage of Negro to total population. In the States concerned a total of 25.8 percent of all persons 15 to 19 years of age and 25.5 percent of all persons 20 to 24 years of age are Negro. The evidence suggests that probably Negroes are proportionately represented on the school aid program, but are under-represented on the college and graduate aid program.

A survey as of December 1937 yields information concerning other characteristics of youth receiving student aid (table 4).[34] A total of 32,979 youth was included in this survey. Two-thirds (22,408) were in receipt of school aid; the remaining one-third (10,571) were receiving college or graduate aid.

TABLE 4.—*Characteristics of youth recipients of student aid, December 1937* [1]

Characteristic	School pupils aided		College and graduate students aided	
	Number	Percent	Number	Percent
Total	22,408	100.0	10,571	100.0
Education:				
High school:				
Less than grade 9	929	4.1		
Grades 9–12	20,866	93.1		
Postgraduate	168	0.8		
Not known	445	2.0		
College:				
Freshman			3,005	28.4
Sophomore			3,033	28.7
Junior			2,144	20.3
Senior			1,853	17.5
Postgraduate			329	3.1
Not known			207	2.0
Sex:				
Male	10,590	47.3	6,337	59.9
Female	11,818	52.7	4,234	40.1
Color:				
White	19,714	88.0	9,902	93.7
Other	2,569	11.5	601	5.7
Not known	125	0.5	68	0.6

[33] U. S. Bureau of the Census, Fifteenth Census of the United States: 1930, Population, vol. II, ch. 10, Age Distribution, table 24, p. 602.

[34] Data compiled by the Works Progress Administration, Division of Research, Statistics, and Records, from NYA Forms 21 and 23, approved application forms for student aid. A 10-percent sampling, subject to revision in the final report dealing with the total group and due to be published about October 1938.

THE STUDENT AID PROGRAM 35

TABLE 4.—*Characteristics of youth recipients of student aid, December 1937* [1]—Continued

Characteristic	School pupils aided		College and graduate students aided	
	Number	Percent	Number	Percent
Specified occupation of parent or guardian:				
Unemployed	4,249	19.0	1,270	2.0
Employed by WPA	2,880	12.8	257	2.4
Professional and technical	277	1.2	959	9.1
Proprietors, managers, and officials	359	1.6	1,077	10.2
Office workers	351	1.6	738	7.0
Sales and kindred workers	421	1.9	829	7.8
Skilled workers	1,811	8.1	1,321	12.5
Semiskilled workers	2,306	10.3	985	9.3
Unskilled workers	2,641	11.8	476	4.5
Domestic and personal service workers	1,623	7.2	591	5.6
Farm operators and laborers	5,271	23.5	1,999	18.9
Not known	219	1.0	69	0.7
Size of family:				
1 or 2	964	4.3		
3 or 4	6,225	27.8		
5 or 6	7,006	31.3		
7 or 8	4,667	20.8		
9 or more	3,406	15.2		
Not known	140	0.6		
Member of a family receiving public relief aid at any time during past 4 years:				
Yes	11,717	52.3		
No	10,317	46.0		
Not known	374	1.7		
Age:				
16	8,026	35.8	122	1.2
17	8,430	37.6	790	7.5
18–19	5,167	23.1	4,137	39.1
20–21	534	2.4	3,452	32.6
22 and older	118	0.5	2,009	19.0
Not known	133	0.6	61	0.6
Number in family who are employed:				
None	4,953	22.1	890	8.4
1	12,726	56.8	6,334	59.9
2	2,861	12.8	2,139	20.3
3 or more	924	4.1	909	8.6
Not known	944	4.2	299	2.8
Yearly family income:				
Less than $400	6,682	29.8	713	6.7
$400–$899	9,164	41.0	2,207	20.9
$900–$1,999	4,087	18.2	5,063	47.9
$2,000–$4,999	185	0.8	1,659	15.7
$5,000 or more	3	0.0	25	0.2
Not known	2,287	10.2	904	8.6

[1] Data compiled by the Works Progress Administration, Division of Research, Statistics, and Records, from NYA Forms 21 and 23, approved application forms for student aid. A 10-percent sampling, subject to revision in the final report dealing with the total group and due to be published about October 1938.

Of the school aid recipients almost all were in grades 9 to 12, slightly less than one-half were males, and slightly more than one-tenth were of races other than white. Approximately three-fourths were 16 or 17 years of age; only 3 percent were older than 19. These youth came predominately from families in financially straitened circumstances. Though about one-fifth of the families had 2 or more members employed, another one-fifth had none employed. Almost all of the pupils came from families in which the yearly income was less than $2,000; about three-tenths, indeed, came from families receiving less than $400 a year. Occupations of all types were represented by the parents or guardians of these children. One-fourth were farm operators or farm laborers; almost one-third were unemployed or on Works Progress Administration rolls; only 6 percent were white-collar workers; and nearly one-fifth were semiskilled or unskilled workers. At some time in the preceding four years at least one-half of all the families concerned had been in receipt of public relief. Large families predominated: One in seven contained 9 persons or more; two-thirds of the families included more than 4 persons each. It is evident that the recipients of high school aid come from underprivileged families, and that therefore, from the point of view of relief alone, the little aid they receive constitutes a justifiable expenditure.

Of the recipients of college and graduate aid in this sampling only 3 percent were graduates; almost three-fifths were freshmen and sophomores. By contrast with the slight predominance of females in the high school group, three-fifths of the college group were males. The proportion of nonwhite persons in the college group was only about one-half that in the high school group. Almost one-fifth of the college youth were over 21 years of age, and less than one-tenth were under 18. More members of the families of these youth were working; in almost three-tenths of the families 2 or more persons were employed, and in less than one-tenth no person was employed. In almost one-sixth of the families the yearly income exceeded $2,000; but more than one-fourth received less than $900 a year. The representation of white-collar workers and skilled artisans was greater in this group than in the high school group, and fewer of the parents were unemployed. In other words, the college youth came from families somewhat better off economically than those of the school aid youth, and probably on the average superior culturally.

Higher Institutions Attended by Recipients of Student Aid

In April 1937 the 23,859 [35] institutions participating in the student aid program included 22,203 schools below college level; 1,469 at the undergraduate college level only; 15 at the graduate level only; and 172 combining both undergraduate and graduate levels.[36] Thus, less than 7 percent (1,656) of all participating institutions were of college grade.

Not all institutions to which quota allotments are made actually participate in the use of such allotments. Furthermore, the allotments for college and graduate aid are made in such a way that the individual institution is allowed discretion in directing the allotment to either the college or graduate level according to the need at any particular time. Consequently, in the analysis which follows, apparent discrepancies between the reported number of institutions to which allotments are made and the number elsewhere officially reported as participating in the program may be understood to reside in the nature of the administration of the program, and do not constitute statistical errors.

For every two public institutions eligible for inclusion in the college aid plan (table 5) there are three private institutions eligible for the same program. Nevertheless, in terms of student quota and the allocation of funds, public institutions are entitled to slightly more than one-half of the total.

Slightly more than one-half of the institutions (table 5) are classified as universities, colleges, or technical schools; less than one-sixth are teachers colleges. The university group receives nearly three-fourths of the student quota and fund allocations; the teachers college group receives about one-sixth, and the junior college group about one-tenth.

---

[35] Cf. revised total reported in table 2, p. 30.
[36] See p. 30, footnote 24.

TABLE 5.—*Institutions participating in the college aid program, by type of institution, student quota, and monthly fund allocation, 1936–37* [1]

Type of institution	Institutions		Student quota		Monthly fund allocation	
	Number	Percent	Number	Percent	Amount	Percent
Total	1,656	100.0	119,219	100.0	$1,768,755	100.0
Public	618	37.3	66,420	55.7	979,168	55.3
Private	995	60.1	52,108	43.7	779,337	44.1
Unknown	43	2.6	691	0.6	10,250	0.6
University, college, or technical school	911	55.0	88,000	73.8	1,315,092	74.4
Teachers college or normal school	263	15.9	18,269	15.3	262,494	14.8
Junior college	439	26.5	12,259	10.3	180,919	10.2
Unknown	43	2.6	691	0.6	10,250	0.6

[1] Compiled by Palmer O. Johnson from replies to NYA Circular Y-40.

On the student aid program at the graduate level, public institutions and private are almost equally divided. Student quotas and the fund allocations are correspondingly equally divided between them.

The College Aid Projects

From reports made in reply to a letter issued from the national office of the Youth Administration in April 1937 it has been possible to prepare a condensed summary descriptive of some of the best types of projects being conducted by youth in the college aid program. An analysis of this sample of 7,083 college aid recipients in 388 colleges reporting yields the distribution of youth according to type of work activity set forth in table 6.

Projects characteristic of the various categories are briefly described below.[38]

Research projects.—Research projects include such activities as soil research, experimentation in ceramics, State historical studies, occupational surveys, the compilation of laws on specific topics, the editing of old manuscripts, the analysis of business trends, the study of building illumination, analyses of delinquency data, the preparation of topographical atlases, and the construction of charts and other devices for instructional use.

[38] Data from replies to NYA Circular Y-50 (April 9, 1937), 2 pp. Mimeographed.

TABLE 6.—*Percentage distribution of 7,083 college aid recipients in 388 colleges, by type of work activity, April 1937* [1]

Type of work activity	Percent of recipients engaged in activity	Type of work activity	Percent of recipients engaged in activity
Total	100.0		
Research, surveys, statistics, etc	21.5	Construction	1.9
Community service	20.5	Recreation and education	1.5
Ground and building maintenance	16.4	Duplication (photography, printing, etc.)	1.3
Departmental service	9.0		
Library service	8.3	Art and dramatics	1.2
Clerical assistance	7.4	Tutorial service	1.1
Laboratory assistance	4.0	Janitorial service	0.9
Home economics	2.8	Miscellaneous	2.4

[1] Data compiled by the NYA from replies to NYA Circular Y-50 (April 9, 1937), 2 pp. Mimeographed.

One illustration of the research type of project is here described. A professor at Connecticut College for Women, New London, supervised a project involving a compilation of all the social welfare laws in force in the State and the recording of day-by-day developments in the field of social legislation in the current sessions of the State legislature. He supervised the work of the three students on the project and directed the classification and indexing of laws and the recording of legislative actions. He also checked the accuracy of work completed.

In addition to receiving financial aid, the students on this project became acquainted with the welfare laws of the State, legislative procedures, and different methods of recording, classifying, and indexing legal materials. The entire project was developed in such a manner as to correlate college aid employment activities with the daily experiences and class work of the students.

The materials now constitute the only available compilation of the social welfare laws of Connecticut in force at the close of the 1936–37 session of the legislature. It is planned to publish the manuscript as a State document, so that social agencies may have copies of the laws under which their activities are carried on.

Community service projects.—Community service projects include such activities as directing play activities in schools, institutions, and public playgrounds; organizing and leading classes in such fields as health, music, and home economics, often under the sponsorship of the Division of Education Projects of the Works Progress Administration; assisting in public libraries; giving practical assistance in the social work aspects of delinquency prevention; organizing community concerts; assisting in public nursery schools; serving as guides and assistants in museums; and assisting public health officers or the officers of other governmental agencies in assembling valuable data and material which otherwise could not have been assembled for governmental use.

Characteristic of community service projects is the following specific illustration: A school for blind persons of white families had been established in Atlanta, Georgia, but none had been established for Negroes. With the cooperation of the principal of the white school, three students receiving aid and attending the Atlanta School of Social Work set out to make some provision for the Negroes. They sought out and listed the names of as many Negro blind as they could find, obtained the use of the basement of a Negro church for their workshop, and formed a committee of citizens to raise funds for the purchase of handicraft material.

Ground and building maintenance.—Ground and building maintenance as carried on in these projects is an activity which in general transcends the drudgery customarily associated with that function. Much of it involves aesthetic improvement, such as landscaping and terracing, and the remodeling of buildings. Some of it, however, is relatively uninspiring, such as the repairing of furniture and windows, the construction of swimming pools, sidewalks, and retaining walls, and the making of signposts.

Illustrative of the activities engaged in in this type of project is the following example. Many trees on the Union College campus at Lincoln, Nebraska, were saved as the result of a project which employed an average of eight students receiving college aid. The students were under the general supervision of the business manager of the college, and under the immediate supervision of one of the group of students in the project who had special training in tree surgery. The scientific treatment of about 50 trees was involved. The decayed sections of the tree trunks were hollowed out and filled with cement to prevent further decay. The campus is located in the midst of a thickly populated suburban section, so that the preserving of the trees has special community value.

"Had it not been for this scientific treatment, nearly all of the trees on our campus would have died," said the director in charge of the project.

Departmental service.—Departmental service bears a very close relationship to the curriculum, and is of direct educational value. It includes such activities as the preparation of supplementary teaching materials; the arrangement of exhibits; the compilation of guides and bibliographies; the classification and cataloguing of documents or museum pieces; the construction of models and technical equipment; and the grading of examinations and the scoring of tests.

The following description of a project is offered as an illustration of this type of work. Under the supervision of a professor in the department of otolaryngology of the Cornell University Medical College, New York City, 10 college aid students constructed, on a scale 50 times natural size, a model of an ear canal, at one end of which was affixed a model otoscope and at the other a typical ear drum. They also prepared 18 models of similar magnification, each representing some disease of the ear drum. The models are used for demonstration purposes.

Library service and clerical projects.—Library service and clerical projects are of such nature as to call for little comment. In the library the essential activities include book repair, cataloguing, stacking, and assisting at the desk; and in clerical work the fundamentals are stenography, typing, filing, and duplicating. Clerical assistance is needed in every department of the institution; and the institution is built around the library. A detailed illustration of these projects is here unnecessary.

Laboratory assistance and home economics assistance.— Laboratory assistance and home economics assistance are similarly so familiar, and yet so essential, as integral functions of American college life as to call for no more than brief comment. In the laboratory youth are employed in such activities as the preparation of specimens, the testing of drinking water, and the analysis of milk. The home economics activities are carried on principally in the cafeteria, although some of the participants are engaged in serving activities of various sorts.

Construction projects.—In construction projects youth make apparatus for general use on the campus, install electric equipment, and construct science units for loan to public schools.

Recreation and education.—Recreation and education activities are extracurricular in nature. They include the direction of intramural activities, the training and development of orchestras, the direction of college socials, and the organization of forums and special groups.

The remaining types of project involve, relatively speaking, too few students to warrant extended consideration here.

Concluding Statement

The school aid program.—The school aid program involves more than nine-tenths of all participating institutions, four-tenths of all funds expended, and almost seven-tenths of all recipients on the entire student aid program. During the year 1936–37 it enabled approximately 280,000 youth [39] to continue their education in approximately 22,000 high schools. It undoubtedly constitutes the major portion of the student aid program.

Unfortunately, far less is known about the detail of the administration of the school aid program and its effectiveness than is known of the college and graduate aid program. So far as can be discovered, youth on the school aid program are less carefully selected, less well supervised, and less consistently followed up than are the older youth on the college

---

[39] Almost 4.4 percent of the 1935–36 total secondary school enrollment, as computed from table 2, p. 30, and data supplied by the U. S. Office of Education.

program. This is especially true of the smaller schools where the supervision of the student aid program has been included among the duties of administrators or teachers who have been unable to give the program the essential supervision it requires.

Despite the lack of detailed accounting, as a commentary on the inadequacy of existing State and local provisions for the continued education of young people at the elementary and high school levels the evidence provided through National Youth Administration records is most impressive. There are presumably at least a quarter of a million young men and women receiving aid to whom on the average less than $5 a month makes all the difference between going to school and not going to school. Yet this quarter of a million constitutes only three-fourths of all applicants for school aid, and there are probably many more youth whose circumstances would warrant aid although their need is not so great. These young people are not incompetents. Though available evidence on their scholastic standing is inadequate, at least it suggests that the recipients of school aid are not inferior to their fellow pupils, and that many of them are employed, for aid received, on jobs which are of real value to the institutions they attend. Nor is the need limited to certain types of community or to relief groups; it exists in representative proportions in communities of all sizes, and is not limited to only extreme poverty.

The provision of free schooling is recognized as a State responsibility. The increased attention of State educational authorities to such types of school functions and problems as the free transportation of pupils, the provision of free textbooks, the raising of the age limit of compulsory school attendance, and the consolidation of schools are evidence of the State's awareness of its responsibility in this connection, and of the tendency to extend the implications of the underlying philosophy of education in a democracy. Consistent with this movement, and in the absence of financial ability on the part of the parents, it would seem reasonable to assume that the State's responsibility should be extended to include provision of the food, clothing, medical services, and school supplies that many school children now lack in adequate amounts.

A number of States apparently do not have the resources to provide these additional services. How far, under such circumstances, the Federal Government can or should go in making provision for them is problematic. But it would seem reasonable to assume that unless the responsibility for providing maintenance for needy students can be assumed by State and local governments—a possibility which at present seems doubtful—some degree of Federal assistance is warranted, and the cost fully justified.

The college and graduate aid program.—Although recognized as a desirable principle, the provision of free educational facilities at the college level for all who can profit therefrom has not yet been accepted as a working practice by the American people. Consequently, although it is well known that the extent of parental wealth and the degree of scholarliness of the children are not directly related, lack of adequate means still constitutes the most effective bar to the enjoyment of educational facilities.

The rendering of financial assistance to worthy students otherwise lacking means has, of course, been practiced for centuries. Individuals and private and public institutions have offered scholarships, awards, and other forms of aid to students who, in the opinion of the authorities, could creditably profit by such assistance. Thus, approved institutions participating in the college and graduate aid program during the academic year 1936–37 reported a total expenditure from their own resources of almost $40,000,000 (at an average of $116 per recipient) in aid to students.

The inadequacy of even this munificent contribution, however, is demonstrated by the fact that almost one and one-half times as many youth applied for college aid on the National Youth Administration program for 1936–37 as were actually granted such aid under the established quota. More than $16,000,000 contributed by the National Youth Administration accommodated nearly 200,000 applicants, for whom as little as $10 to $15 a month made all the difference between attending college and not attending college. Obviously there is still a vast reservoir of potential college material which existing institutions have not tapped, but which, if the excellent record already established by recipients of college aid may be accepted as a criterion, is probably in large part competent to profit by education at the college level.

The college and graduate aid program requires that students participating shall be employed, in return for aid, on projects of value to the institution or the community and, so far as possible, directly related to the student's educational needs. Thus even the *quid pro quo* becomes a part of the entire educational service, and the student retains his self-respect.

By establishing the college and graduate aid program on a need and ability basis rather than on a relief basis, the National Youth Administration has only the more clearly recognized and made the public aware of the fact that education even at the higher levels is warranted not as charity but as a profitable social investment. The college undergraduate and graduate aid programs of the Youth Administration have provided large numbers of young men and women with an opportunity to continue their education. As a result the number of persons on the labor market has been considerably reduced.

The National Youth Administration has vested in the institutions themselves the responsibility for the selection of students, the determination of policy, and the administration of the program. The policy of placing the administration of the college and graduate aid program in the hands of college officials has, on the whole, been advantageous to the National Youth Administration and to the colleges. Administrative costs have thus been reduced to a minimum and the institutions have been freed from direct or implied interference with their educational programs. The policy has demonstrated not only the possibility of harmonious working relations between governmental agencies and institutions of higher education, but also the extent to which, given charge of public funds to disburse for that purpose, those institutions can be entrusted to administer a college aid program economically and effectively.

In those institutions where the college and graduate aid programs have been carefully planned and executed, experience on student aid projects, when correlated with the field of study, has had distinct educational value to the youth employed. Similarly, where projects have been carefully planned and supervised, the outcomes have been of substantial value to institutions and to those communities in which college youth have worked on community projects. College administrators, student beneficiaries, the State youth directors, and chief State school officers are generally agreed that the college and graduate aid program has been beneficial to students and to institutions.

At this point it seems pertinent to consider two questions which have raised doubts in the minds of some critics of the college aid program. First, should the Federal Government grant student aid to persons attending institutions that are not publicly controlled? And, second, should the regulations of the National Youth Administration permit States to restrict the list of approved institutions to those with adequate educational standards?

On the issue of publicly versus privately controlled institutions, the attitude of the Federal Government as expressed through the National Youth Administration is consistent, simple, and clear. Student aid is extended not to institutions but to individuals; it is Federal aid to the needy. In view of the fact, however, that the work performed by the youth in return for aid is of benefit to the institution concerned, only those educational institutions that operate on a non-profit-making basis may be considered as eligible for participation on the Federal aid program. On this understanding it is obvious that, provided both student and institution comply with the regulations, there is no warranty for discrimination between public and private control. Whatever institutions are approved by the State as tax-exempt, non-profit-making, bona fide educational institutions are ipso facto acceptable to the National Youth Administration.

On the question of adequate educational standards, the Federal regulations neither affirm nor deny the right of the State to refuse certification for student aid to institutions which, although otherwise in conformity with regulation requirements, nevertheless fall below certain standards of quality. In other words, the National Youth Administration presumably gives the State no right to discriminate between institutions as regards quality except to the extent necessary to establish the bona fide educational character of those certified. That the Federal Government cannot properly speaking set itself up as an accrediting agency is obvious; but that it should not specifically make it optional for the States to refuse certification is perhaps unfortunate, especially in view of the fact that under existing regulations many institutions may be and have been certified which actually are unable to meet the requirements of any established accrediting agency.

CHAPTER IV
THE WORK PROJECTS PROGRAM

This chapter constitutes a consideration of the nature and scope of the work projects program, the characteristics of the youth employed on the projects, the educational provisions made for them, and the kinds of projects in which they are engaged.

Nature and Scope
of the Program [1]

The work projects program of the National Youth Administration commenced in January 1936 [2] and was designed primarily for the purpose of providing work relief for young men and women 16 to 24 years of age. But, because of the nature of the compulsory school attendance laws in certain States, the inadequacy of available funds to provide work for all unemployed youth, the difficulties of placing the younger members of the youth group in employment, and the general attitude of the Federal Government and some of the State governments concerning the special safeguards which should surround the employment of children under 18 years of age, in August 1936 the lower age limit was raised to 18. [3]

Preference in employment is given to youth whose need for relief has been certified by some public relief agency approved by the Works Progress Administration. According to regulations, and unless otherwise authorized, at least 90 percent of all workers on a youth project must be youth having relief status; the remaining 10 percent, whether supervisors or regular employees, may consist of youth and adults of nonrelief status.

---

[1] Unless otherwise indicated, the contents of this section refer to conditions under the 1937–38 program. See Procedure for the Planning and Operation of National Youth Administration Sponsored Nation-Wide Projects, NYA Bulletin No. 8 (July 9, 1937), 16 pp. Mimeographed.

[2] Procedure for the Development and Operation of National Youth Administration Sponsored Federal Projects, NYA Bulletin No. 4 (January 3, 1936), 11 pp. Mimeographed.

[3] Works Progress Administration, Administrative Order No. 46 (August 21, 1936), and NYA Bulletin No. 8.

Until recently the assignment and classification of youth labor on youth projects was made by the Division of Employment of the Works Progress Administration.[4] All enrollees on work projects are required to maintain active registration with public employment offices designated by the United States Employment Service, and are given every encouragement to accept employment in private industry.

Other than for supervisory and administrative employees, the working hours of youth on work projects are limited to 8 per day, 40 per week, and 70 per month. Hourly wage rates are established by the State youth director in collaboration with the State Works Progress Administration director; but no relief youth employee may earn more than $25 per month. At least 75 percent of the funds allotted to a State for youth projects must be expended as wages for the certified relief youth there employed.

Although the State youth director is the official sponsor for all youth work projects, most projects are also sponsored by some public, quasi-public, or non-profit-making agency in cooperation with the Youth Administration. The contributions of these cosponsors are generally in the form of supervision, services, funds, or the provision of equipment and materials.

Application to establish a youth work project is made jointly by the sponsoring agencies. The official application form calls for information on the following items: The location of the project; a description of the project and the character of the work involved; the expected dates of commencement and completion of the project; an estimate of the number of workers to be employed, analyzed by occupation and degree of skill; an estimate of expected costs in terms of labor, supervision, travel, materials, etc.; and the qualifications of the project supervisor.

Ordinarily, approval of an application for the establishment of a youth work project is the responsibility of the State youth director alone, but copies of approved applications are filed with the national office. Because of their special

---

[4] By Administrative Order No. 60 of the Works Progress Administration, January 12, 1938, the responsibility and authority for certification through existing public agencies has been transferred to the State youth director, subject to approval by the Works Progress Administration regional social worker. This policy was adopted to accelerate the certification of youth.

significance, however, the following types of project must be submitted to the national office for endorsement before final approval: Building construction projects in which the value of materials required exceeds $500; resident agricultural training projects; and statistical, survey, and research projects. The last-mentioned type is scrutinized by the Statistical Review Section (formerly called Coordinating Committee) of the Works Progress Administration, a function of which is to assess the scientific value of all projects of this nature and to ascertain that each proposed study complies with acceptable standards of scientific investigation.

In judging the value of a project the following criteria are used: The number of youth to be employed, the expected duration of the project, the types of work on which the youth will be employed, and the benefits that may be expected to accrue to the youth and the local community as a result of the establishment of the project.

The proper conduct of each established project is the responsibility of the project supervisor. He in turn is subordinate to the district supervisor, who reports to the State director. Thus the State office maintains constant supervision over all of its youth work projects. A project may be terminated at any time the State director sees fit.

Formerly the Youth Administration approved only the following types of youth work projects: Community development and recreational leadership, rural development, public service, and research. Since July 1937, however, the program has been conducted as a single Nation-wide official project, sponsored by the National Youth Administration, and comprising a large number of work activities of various types, a brief classification of which follows:

I. Construction work:
    1. Highway, road, and street projects:
        a. Roadside improvements, trails, footpaths, etc.
        b. Other highway, road, and street projects.
    2. Public building projects:
        a. Construction of new buildings.
        b. Remodeling and repair of public buildings.
        c. Improvement of grounds around buildings.
    3. Recreational facilities, exclusive of buildings.
    4. Conservation work.

THE WORK PROJECTS PROGRAM 51

II. Nonconstruction work:
   1. Nursery schools.
   2. Clerical and stenographic work:
      a. For governmental agencies.
      b. For other than governmental agencies.
   3. Resident agricultural training projects.
   4. Agricultural demonstration projects (county agent assistance, etc.)
   5. School lunches.
   6. Library service and book repairing.
   7. Homemaking.
   8. Museum work, preparation of exhibits, visual aid materials, etc.
   9. Statistical and nonstatistical survey and research projects.
   10. Recreational leadership projects.
   11. Fine arts (art, music, drama, writing).
   12. Sewing.
III. Miscellaneous work:
   1. Educational camps for unemployed women (since discontinued).
   2. Workshops (handicrafts, toy making and repair, furniture construction, etc.)
   3. Youth center activities (not elsewhere classified).
   4. Other National Youth Administration work (not elsewhere classified).

Funds for the development of the work projects program for the employment of out-of-school youth who are members of families certified for employment under the Works Progress Administration were first made available in November 1935. The amount expended by the National Youth Administration on the work projects program during the latter half of the fiscal year 1935–36 totaled approximately $15,000,000.[5] The average total expenditure per youth employed on this program for this period approximated $134.[6] For the entire fiscal year 1936–37 a sum of approximately $35,500,000 was expended on National Youth Administration work projects.[7] The average total expenditure per youth employed for this year approximated $225.[8]

For the fiscal year 1937–38 the National Youth Administration work projects program has been allotted the sum of approximately $31,000,000.[9]

---

[5] See p. 17.
[6] Information supplied by the NYA.
[7] See p. 17.
[8] See p. 18.
[9] See p. 17.

The Youth Employed

The number of youth employed on work projects operated by the National Youth Administration varies somewhat from month to month. The median monthly total employed during the calendar year 1936 was 161,306; during the calendar year 1937 it was 171,207. A detailed listing of monthly totals since January 1936 is presented in table 7, which indicates the breakdown according to relief status. It will be noted that the number of nonrelief youth constitutes only a small fraction of the total.

TABLE 7.—*Youth employed on work projects, by relief status, sex, and month, January 1936 to November 1937* [1]

Year and month	Total number	Certified as in need of relief		Males	
		Number	Percent	Number	Percent
1936:					
January	15,890	15,588	98.1	9,620	60.5
February	74,884	73,730	98.5	45,381	60.6
March	159,130	156,381	98.3	95,021	59.7
April	176,344	172,996	98.1	102,580	58.2
May	173,004	169,484	97.9	96,830	56.0
June	179,399	175,270	97.7	97,917	54.6
July	160,183	155,678	97.2	85,726	53.5
August	157,065	153,118	97.5	82,596	52.6
September	161,903	158,072	97.6	84,930	52.5
October	160,709	157,251	97.8	82,376	51.3
November	166,880	163,231	97.8	84,370	50.6
December	172,221	168,578	97.9	87,882	51.0
1937:					
January	178,679	174,935	97.9	91,857	51.4
February	182,497	178,312	97.7	93,978	51.5
March	184,561	180,763	97.9	94,716	51.3
April	184,727	181,300	98.1	93,294	50.5
May	177,008	173,825	98.2	86,045	48.6
June	165,407	162,435	98.2	78,911	47.7
July	143,707	141,170	98.2	67,397	46.9
August	127,331	125,122	98.3	59,504	46.7
September	121,915	119,799	98.3	56,544	46.4
October	118,184	116,278	98.4	54,375	46.0
November	122,402	120,488	98.4	56,476	46.1

[1] Number of Youths and Adults Employed on Projects Operated by the National Youth Administration, by Relief Status and by Month, January 1936 through November 1937, Works Progress Administration, Division of Research, Statistics, and Records, NYA Series R-1202 (January 25, 1938), tables 1-2.

An analysis of wages received and hours worked by 175,538 relief youth employed on youth work projects during May 1937 [10] indicates that these youth worked a total of 7,459,631

---

[10] The discrepancy between this total and that reported in table 7 is attributable to the fact that at the time of initial reporting for any month accurate data are not available. See appendix B, table 5, for breakdown by States.

hours for a total wage of $2,581,737. The average hourly wage was $0.35; average monthly earnings totaled $14.71 per youth employed. Considerable variation obtains among the States.

During the period 1936–37, the average Federal expenditure per youth employed on work projects approximated $225 per annum.[11] The average monthly wage per youth employed was approximately $15.

The distribution by sex of the youth employed on youth work projects has changed noticeably since the program began. The proportion of males to all youth employed gradually declined from 61 percent in January 1936 to 46 percent in October 1937 (table 7); recently, however, the percentage of males has shown signs of increase. An explanation of this development is as follows: In the beginning of the program the chief objective was to get jobs for boys. Many had been enrolled in the Civilian Conservation Corps; others were enrolled on National Youth Administration work projects, and attempts were made to find jobs for them in private industry. For a while girls were a relatively minor consideration. As conditions in private industry improved, the proportion of boys on the youth projects program diminished. Meanwhile a vast reservoir of certified but unemployed girls had been accumulating. As the demand for jobs among boys became less urgent, that for girls became more urgent. Furthermore, the relief certification agencies were so occupied in dealing with the adult relief problem that they had little opportunity to devote much time to youth. Consequently, they tended to neglect the certification of new youth cases, and left the National Youth Administration to draw upon the existing reservoir. Recent improvements (since November 1937) in the working relationship between the National Youth Administration and the relief certification agencies [12] are replenishing the reservoir of registered unemployed youth, with the result that boys are once more being employed on National Youth Administra-

---

[11] Including both national and State administrative costs and all Federal contributions in materials, etc. Cf. p. 18.

[12] See p. 49, footnote 4.

tion work projects in a proportion more nearly commensurate with their representation in the population at large.

No comprehensive survey has been made of the characteristics of work project youth. Consequently, for information on age, color or race, education, size of family, reasons for leaving school, vocational training, and previous work experience, it has been found necessary to depend on such incidental reports during the year 1936–37 as could be obtained through request from the national office to the State directors.[13] Obviously it is impossible, on the basis of such scant evidence, to claim more than merely suggestive indications of the characteristics of project youth. To attempt to correlate the information and make any more than the most elementary deductions from it would be unwarranted. The need for more extensive data of this nature is imperative.

An analysis of reports from California, Nebraska, and Ohio, relating to conditions after August 1936, when the lower age limit for youth on work projects was raised from 16 to 18, indicates that, out of 6,697 youth employed, 14 percent were 18 years old, 25 percent were 19 years old, 20 percent were 20 years old, 15 percent were 21 years old, and 26 percent were 22 years old or older.

Out of 26,180 youth employed on projects in seven States [14] and New York City, 89 percent were white. In Louisiana and Kentucky alone the percentage was 87. In a sample of 126 projects [15] it was found that 88 percent of the youth employed were white.

Project youth come from large families. Out of 19,306 youth in five States,[16] 9 percent came from families of only 1 or 2 persons, 28 percent from families of 3 or 4 persons, 29 percent from 5- or 6-person families, and 34 percent from families of 7 persons or more.

---

[13] Letter of August 6, 1937. Replies which were of use in whole or in part in the present connection were received from California, Kansas, Kentucky, Louisiana, Michigan, Minnesota, Nebraska, New Hampshire, New York City, Ohio, and West Virginia. Data relate to various periods during 1936 and 1937. It should be noted that not all of these States made complete returns. For example, the data for Ohio refer to only one district.

[14] California, Louisiana, Kentucky, Michigan, Minnesota, Nebraska, Ohio.

[15] For a discussion of these projects, see pp. 69 ff.

[16] California, Kentucky, Nebraska, New York City, Ohio.

A sample of 35,638 youth on work projects in 8 States [17] and New York City reveals that one-half had no more than 8 years of schooling, almost one-half had 9 to 12 years, and 3 percent had more than 12 years. A sample of 13,547 of these youth in four States [18] indicates that, among the various reasons given for leaving school, financial difficulties ranked first (47 percent); discouragement and lack of interest, second (24 percent); and graduation from high school, third (13 percent). Information concerning vocational training is exceedingly sketchy. Out of 11,367 work project youth in California and Kentucky 68 percent had had no vocational training.

A study of 19,808 youth (of whom slightly more than one-half were boys) employed on youth work projects in six States [19] indicates (table 8) that prior to employment on the project 33 percent had had no previous work experience; 17 percent (almost all boys) had engaged in some form of unskilled labor; 10 percent (similarly almost all boys) had worked on farms; 14 percent (almost all girls) had been employed as household, domestic, or personal servants; 11 percent had worked in what may be termed white-collar occupations; and 10 percent had had experience in skilled or semiskilled work, principally in factories. A marked predominance of unskilled and semiskilled work experience among the two-thirds able to report any previous experience at all is characteristic of these youth.

The extent to which experience on work projects has increased the employability of the youth there employed is difficult to determine. There can be little question that the work projects operate to compensate for one of the most serious deficiencies reported by the youth themselves, namely, lack of work experience. On the other hand, it is perhaps reasonable to evaluate the work performed on projects as exploratory experience, contributing to the orientation of the youthful worker, rather than to the development of specific skills. It is significant, however,

---

[17] California, Kansas, Kentucky, Minnesota, Nebraska, New Hampshire, Ohio, West Virginia.

[18] California, Kentucky, Minnesota, Ohio.

[19] California, Kentucky, Michigan, Minnesota, Ohio, West Virginia.

that out of 164,240 youth leaving youth projects during the 10-month period February through November 1937, almost one-third entered private employment and 7 percent entered

TABLE 8.—*Previous work experience of 19,808 work project youth prior to National Youth Administration employment, by type of work and sex* [1]

Type of work	Work project youth reporting							
	Total		Males		Females		Unclassified as to sex [2]	
	Number	Percent	Number	Percent	Number	Percent	Number	Percent
Total	19,808	100.0	10,171	100.0	7,976	100.0	1,661	100.0
CCC, WPA, and PWA [3]	89	0.4	76	0.7	13	0.2		
Public service	5	0.0	5	0.0				
Unskilled labor	3,129	15.8	2,261	22.2	373	4.7	495	29.8
Farming	2,006	10.2	1,994	19.6	12	0.2		
Mining	214	1.1	214	2.1				
Lumbering	21	0.1	21	0.2				
Household, domestic, and personal service [3]	2,696	13.6	217	2.1	1,993	25.0	486	29.3
Sales clerks and agents	833	4.2	375	3.7	458	5.7		
Office	1,218	6.1	175	1.7	657	8.2	386	23.2
Factory and semiskilled	1,143	5.8	479	4.7	416	5.2	248	14.9
Crafts and skilled	883	4.5	634	6.2	213	2.7	36	2.2
Professional and kindred	215	1.1	58	0.6	147	1.8	10	0.6
No work experience reported	6,441	32.5	2,984	29.5	3,457	43.3		
No information given	915	4.6	678	6.7	237	3.0		

[1] Data for California, Kentucky, Michigan, Minnesota, Ohio, West Virginia. See p. 54, footnote 13.
[2] Data for Michigan were not classified as to sex.
[3] In the case of the Ohio reports, these three categories are not mutually exclusive.

Government employment (table 9).[20] One-tenth left because no longer technically eligible; about 6 in 100 (almost all girls) left to marry; about one-tenth left because their jobs on the project expired; fewer than 3 in 100 were dismissed for inefficiency; only 3 in 100 left to return to school; and more than one-fourth left for various miscellaneous reasons or for reasons unknown.

[20] Replies to NYA Circular Y-45 (February 25, 1937), 2 pp. Mimeographed.

TABLE 9.—*Number of youth leaving National Youth Administration work projects, by reason for leaving, February to November, 1937* [1]

Reason for leaving	Total youth leaving		Number of youth leaving, by month									
	Number	Percent	February	March	April	May	June	July	August	September	October	November
All reasons	164,240	100.0	9,141	12,592	17,521	24,489	26,268	24,906	12,905	14,203	12,500	9,715
Private employment:												
Permanent	30,599	18.6	2,115	2,619	3,837	5,483	4,591	2,931	2,114	2,828	2,342	1,739
Seasonal or temporary	17,256	10.5	537	1,754	2,795	2,527	2,746	2,275	1,484	1,274	1,094	770
Doubtful or not ascertained	5,417	3.3	325			720	1,057	1,018	737	666	627	266
Governmental work:												
Normal	891	0.5	31	93	124	174	115	100	44	50	70	90
Emergency	10,887	6.5	709	937	2,299	1,640	819	725	580	487	1,226	1,165
School attendance	4,685	2.9	132	162	153	262	196	98	247	2,047	1,083	305
Ineligibility or end of need	18,830	11.5	1,062	1,465	1,892	2,647	4,225	3,250	1,562	1,097	770	860
No job or program	17,470	10.6	751	274	309	3,381	3,385	6,670	1,103	806	353	438
Inefficiency	4,455	2.7	421	517	490	488	720	610	380	353	235	241
Marriage	9,522	5.8	509	764	1,090	1,197	1,734	1,189	767	754	802	716
Other or unknown	44,529	27.1	2,549	4,007	4,532	5,970	6,680	6,040	3,887	3,841	3,898	3,125

[1] Replies to NYA Circular Y-45 (February 25, 1937), 2 pp. Mimeographed.

Though the above analysis of reasons for terminating employment on work projects indicates that a substantial proportion of the turn-over is accounted for by the absorption of youth in private employment, much of the work thus provided is of a seasonal or temporary character. Furthermore, of the youth employed by governmental departments, the vast majority entered the service of emergency agencies. It is, therefore, open to question to what extent these youth are permanently absorbed in employment and thus removed from the vast reservoir of unemployed.

Evidence relating to duration of employment on youth work projects as of March 1937 is available in a Works Progress Administration report (table 10).[21] Out of 186,630 certified youth employed,[22] almost one-fifth had been only intermittently employed since first assignment. By contrast, one-fourth had been continuously employed for a year or more. The median for the group represents a period of continuous employment of approximately 4.6 months. The duration of employment varies, however, with the wage class in which employed. The unskilled class had been in employment a median period of 3.7 months, the professional and technical 5.9 months, the intermediate 7.2 months, and the skilled 7.6 months.

Adequate evidence to explain the observed differences in duration of employment between wage classes is not available, although a partial explanation is possible. First, the wage class designations refer not to the abilities of the youth employed, but rather to the type of work on which they were employed. Second, in the spring and summer of 1936 most projects called for unskilled workers. Since that date many projects of this type have been closed, and greater emphasis has been placed on projects calling for higher degrees of skill. Construction projects seldom last long. Third, it has been the custom on youth work projects to classify most newcomers as unskilled, and to move them up to higher levels as they demonstrate their ability; in this connection it is interesting to note that the unskilled in March 1937 constituted only two-thirds of the total.

---

[21] Employment on NYA Projects, by Duration of Employment * * * Works Progress Administration, Division of Research, Statistics and Records, R-917 (May 27, 1937), tables 1-3.

[22] Compare revised total reported in table 7, p. 52.

TABLE 10.—*Duration of employment of relief youth since first assignment on work projects, by wage class, March 1937* [1]

Duration of employment	Total relief youth employed		Relief youth employed, by wage class							
			Unskilled		Intermediate		Skilled		Professional and technical	
	Number	Percent	Number	Percent	Number	Percent	Number	Percent	Number	Percent
Total	186,630	100.0	123,613	100.0	49,160	100.0	12,853	100.0	1,004	100.0
Not continuously employed	34,433	18.4	24,463	19.8	7,782	15.8	1,983	15.4	205	20.4
Continuously employed	152,197	81.6	99,150	80.2	41,378	84.2	10,870	84.6	799	79.6
1-2 months	28,676	18.8	22,435	22.6	4,995	12.1	1,139	10.5	107	13.4
3-5 months	35,383	23.2	26,629	26.9	6,833	16.5	1,789	16.5	132	16.5
6-8 months	21,844	14.4	13,210	13.3	6,709	16.2	1,778	16.3	147	18.4
9-11 months	18,402	12.1	10,643	10.7	6,096	14.7	1,540	14.2	123	15.4
12 months and over	47,892	31.5	26,233	26.5	16,745	40.5	4,624	42.5	290	36.3

[1] Employment on NYA Projects, by Duration of Employment * * * Works Progress Administration, Division of Research, Statistics, and Records, R-917 (May 27, 1937), tables 1-3. Omitted from this table are 5,038 nonrelief youth.

TABLE 11.—*Duration of employment of work project youth since first assignment, by type of community, March 1937* [1]

Duration of employment	Total youth employed		Youth employed, by size of largest city in county of residence							
			Under 2,500		2,500 to 9,999		10,000 to 99,999		100,000 and over	
	Number	Percent	Number	Percent	Number	Percent	Number	Percent	Number	Percent
Total	191,668	100.0	34,072	100.0	36,690	100.0	52,909	100.0	67,997	100.0
Not continuously employed	34,764	18.1	6,112	17.9	7,726	21.1	10,183	19.2	10,743	15.8
Continuously employed	156,904	81.9	27,960	82.1	28,964	78.9	42,726	80.8	57,254	84.2
1–2 months	29,265	18.6	6,366	22.8	6,641	22.9	8,070	18.9	8,188	14.3
3–5 months	36,182	23.1	6,668	23.8	7,156	24.7	9,945	23.3	12,413	21.7
6–8 months	22,777	14.5	4,131	14.8	4,533	15.7	6,381	14.9	7,732	13.5
9–11 months	18,911	12.1	2,412	8.6	3,275	11.3	5,470	12.8	7,754	13.5
12 months and over	49,769	31.7	8,383	30.0	7,359	25.4	12,860	30.1	21,167	37.0

[1] See p. 59, table 10, footnote 1.

Evidence is also available, relating to March 1937, concerning the distribution of work project youth in terms of urban-rural residence (table 11). Out of 191,668 youth employed on youth work projects at that date, including 5,038 nonrelief wage youth, 18 percent came from counties distinctly rural, 19 percent from counties with village and small-town communities, 28 percent from counties with medium-sized towns and small cities, and 35 percent from counties with large cities. This distribution coincides fairly closely with that of the total population of the United States.

The median duration of employment in the urban counties is 5 months and in rural counties 4 months. In counties with small cities of 2,500 to 9,999 population it is only 3 months. The percentage of youth not continuously employed is least in rural counties and in counties with large cities.

Some indication of the type of work done by youth on work projects, and of the proportionate emphasis placed on each type, may be derived from a study of table 12, which presents data on the number of youth employed on various kinds of projects as of October 1937. By recombining items in terms of type of work instead of type of project the following general conclusions may be drawn: Almost three-tenths of the youth were employed in labor on building and road projects (items 1, 2, 3); two-tenths were engaged in clerical and statistical work (items 7, 9); another two-tenths were employed in home economics activities, principally sewing (items 5a, 12a, 13a, 13b); about one-tenth were engaged in arts and crafts or library and museum services (items 8a, 8b, 10, 12b); another one-tenth were employed in work involving recreational leadership (item 6); and a final one-tenth were engaged in miscellaneous activities (items 4, 5b, 8c, 11, 13c). It is obvious that few of these youth are employed at work which calls for a high degree of skill or training.

The Work Projects

The wide range of activities in which youth are engaged on the National Youth Administration work projects, and the diversified nature of the projects themselves, make it impossible to present an adequate description of this major phase of the National Youth Administration program. Consequently, the present section will be devoted to, first, a general analysis of data relating to a sampling of 126 "outstanding" project descriptions taken at random from

TABLE 12.—*Distribution of youth employed on work projects, by type of project, October 1937* [1]

Type of project	Youth employed	
	Number	Percent
Total [2]	119,035	100.00
1. Highways, roads, and streets:		
a. Roadside improvements, trails, etc.	2,138	1.80
b. Other	1,964	1.65
2. Public buildings:		
a. New construction	3,335	2.80
b. Remodeling and repairs	3,155	2.65
c. Improvement of grounds	6,426	5.40
3. Recreational facilities (excluding buildings)	16,134	13.55
4. Conservation	1,413	1.19
5. Education:		
a. Nursery schools	2,527	2.12
b. Resident agricultural training	1,089	0.92
6. Recreational leadership	13,833	11.62
7. Clerical:		
a. For governmental agencies	19,642	16.50
b. For nongovernmental agencies	3,802	3.19
8. Professional and technical:		
a. Library service and book repair	5,804	4.88
b. Museum exhibit and visual aid	761	0.64
c. Agricultural demonstration	1,908	1.60
9. Survey and research	310	0.26
10. Fine arts	906	0.76
11. Youth center activities	2,130	1.79
12. Goods:		
a. Sewing	13,052	10.97
b. Workshops	6,929	5.82
13. Miscellaneous:		
a. School lunches	812	0.68
b. Homemaking	4,469	3.75
c. Other N Y A work	6,496	5.46

[1] Employment, Hours and Earnings on Work Projects of the National Youth Administration . . . Month Ending October 31, 1937. Works Progress Administration, Division of Research, Statistics, and Records R-1146 (December 16, 1937). Cf. revised total in table 7.
[2] Excluding Michigan for which detail by type of project is not available.

the monthly reports of State directors filed in the national office during the year 1936–37; second, a brief description of some of the more significant types of work in which the youth are engaged; and third, a summary of a report by the Works Progress Administration engineering division evaluating specifically the National Youth Administration construction projects.

THE WORK PROJECTS PROGRAM

Analysis of a sample of 126 "outstanding" projects.[24]—The types of work project carried on during the year 1936–37, on the basis of a sample of 126 "outstanding" projects, are as follows:

  1. Construction, repair, and remodeling of public buildings, and the improvement of public grounds.
  2. Construction, repair, and improvement of highways, roads, footpaths, and trails.
  3. Preparation of recreational parks and areas.
  4. Recreational leadership.
  5. Library and museum service.
  6. Clerical, statistical, and research work on public service projects.
  7. Workshop projects.
  8. Agricultural demonstration, conservation of natural resources, and resident agricultural training projects.
  9. Home economics projects, including sewing, nursery schools, nursing aides, and school lunches.

Out of the total of 126 projects only 2 had no cosponsor and only 1 was sponsored by a division of the Federal Government.[25] But 17 different kinds of State department, 16 different kinds of county agency, and 24 different kinds of city or township agency or office participated alone or jointly with others as sponsors; and of quasi-public agencies, there were 12 different kinds which assumed the role of cosponsor. It would thus appear that local governmental agencies are the most likely to encourage and establish youth projects. This observation illustrates the policy of the national office of operating in every possible way through existing local agencies and by means of decentralized control.

The variety of specific activities in which youth are engaged on these 126 projects yields a total of approximately 175 specific unclassified items.[26]

Conservation projects.—Following the recommendations of the Upstream Engineering Conference in Washington during September 1936, the National Youth Administration joined with other State and Federal forces in promoting the cause of conservation throughout the country. Thousands of

---
[24] Compiled by P. O. Johnson from replies to NYA Circular Y-45.
[25] See appendix C.
[26] See appendix D.

National Youth Administration project workers have been engaged in tasks of many kinds designed to preserve forests, to prevent farm lands from erosion, and to return to productive use lands that have been despoiled.

National Youth Administration project workers are performing soil conservation work in a number of Southern and Midwestern States. In Texas alone, under the sponsorship of the Agricultural Extension Service, these youth have run terracing lines on more than 500,000 acres of farm lands, demonstrating to farmers how they can protect their soil from washing and blowing away. In one district in Kansas youth on work projects have assisted in running contour lines on 14,979 acres of land. Of this number, 3,820 are pasture acres and 11,159 are cropland acres. The youth also planted over 13,000 trees and shrubs.

Elsewhere they are collecting rainfall and run-off data, constructing small check dams and retaining walls, planting cover crops and tree seedlings, developing recreation areas, building game refuges and fish hatcheries, and in many other ways promoting the general cause of conservation of the Nation's resources. In the Dakotas, Missouri, and Oklahoma, for instance, and in many other States, youth on work projects are assisting in the restoration of the natural life which has been destroyed during the past years.

In addition to the values to the communities of the work which they perform, the youth on these projects have learned the importance of soil conservation and of the extension of conservation practices to the smaller streams and watersheds which feed the main drainage basins of the country.

Projects in highway and wayside park beautification.—The first highway park and roadside beautification project was started in Texas during January 1936. Before the end of that year, highway projects were in operation throughout the State. At the peak of this program approximately 2,000 youth were employed and approximately 150 wayside parks had been built along the highways of the State. The youth employed also did road work; flattened slopes, filled ditches, and sodded shoulders and slopes; constructed ditch retards and check dams; painted guard fences and signposts; cleaned and drained ditches; planted, trimmed, and cultivated trees and shrubs; gravelled and widened side-road approaches, and gravelled mailbox turnouts, road shoulders, and school bus stops; constructed native stone retaining walls; landscaped highways at entrances to towns and cities; constructed highway sidewalks; and constructed nurseries and erected greenhouses for the growth of plants to be transplanted to highway projects.

Clerical projects.—About 300 specially selected work project youth have been employed in the Ellis Island and Washington Street offices of the Bureau of Immigration and Naturalization of New York City. Through their help a serious arrearage in the work of the Immigration Bureau has been substantially reduced, and officials at the Bureau have stated that the files and records are in better condition than they had been for some time.

The Immigration Bureau project has always experienced a large turn-over of personnel to outside jobs. Most of these jobs are for the same type of work that the young persons have been doing on the project, and are well above the level of positions usually found by workers leaving other projects. This successful job placement may be due to the fact that National Youth Administration employees are carefully selected and are expected to turn out as high grade work as the Bureau's own civil service employees. There is no discrimination against the work project youth, and no distinction is made between the regular employees of the Bureau and the National Youth Administration part-time workers.

Resident agricultural training projects.—Through another National Youth Administration activity planned on a Nation-wide basis, agricultural and homemaking courses are now being made available to youth who are members of tenant and low-income farm families. These projects, which commenced in April 1937, are conducted in cooperation with the Department of Agriculture and various State agricultural schools and colleges. The period of employment ranges from 1 to 6 months, depending upon the type of program developed in the particular locality. Tuition consumes approximately half of the employee's time.

Tuition, subsistence, and other costs are worked out on the project. Total costs may not exceed $35 a month, of which only $5 goes to the youth. The remainder pays for his board and lodging in the dormitories of the institution sponsoring the project.[27]

Young persons are selected for resident agricultural training projects on the basis of eligibility for National Youth Administration employment and ability to profit by the type of training offered. They are assigned in groups as special students with courses of study adapted to their particular needs and educational levels. The bulk of the training for boys is given through demonstration in such fields as farm practice, soil conservation, soil chemistry, dairying, poultry raising, crop diversification, and care of farm equipment. Girls are trained in home maintenance and in the principles of cooking, economical marketing, home gardening, and canning and perservation of foods. There are about 70 of these agricultural and vocational residence training projects now in operation and the program is rapidly extending.[28]

Workshop projects.—The establishment of workshops as projects employing National Youth Administration youth has developed rapidly throughout the country. This type of project is particularly well adapted to rural sections of the country where equipment and supplies for rural schools are needed and can easily be made. Recreational equipment, such as benches, fountains, basketball backstops, and tennis nets, is also made by these youth. The following examples will serve to illustrate the work youth are performing in workshop projects.

In the State of Arkansas workshops have been established in many sections. For example, in the small town of Friendship, Hot Spring County, both boys and girls have been assigned to a workshop project. From raw materials donated by the community the boys are making split-bottom chairs to be used by schools and other public agencies. The girls do the weaving of the bottoms as the chairs are completed. The youth are being taught the use of hand tools,

---

[27] WPA News Release No. 6-249, February 8, 1938, p. 8, and data supplied by the NYA.
[28] WPA News Release No. 6-249, p. 8.

the reading of simple blueprints, and other activities that are closely allied to this type of project.

The State of Kentucky has made excellent use of the workshop in the rural mountainous areas, and has produced many articles of furniture for use in rural schools. For example, a manual craft workshop project in Wayne County has employed youth in the production of chairs, tables, and cabinets, which were turned over to the county board of education, the cosponsor of the project. The county board furnished all materials and the building in which the project was housed. The equipment consisted mostly of home-made and improvised lathes, ripsaws, presses, workbenches, and tools. The source of power was an abandoned 3-horsepower engine. During 1 month alone, 270 articles were finished and turned over to the sponsor. Training in the use of machinery, the cutting and assembling of furniture from rough lumber, and the tempering of steel has already enabled these youth to make furniture for their own homes and, on occasion, to sell small pieces made after project hours.

Another project in Morgan County, Kentucky, a strictly rural county, employs youth in making library tables, bookcases, library chairs, high school table-arm chairs, and kindergarten chairs—all to be used in the rural public schools of the county. Here again the cosponsor is the county board of education.

Workshop projects of various kinds are in operation in Maine, Maryland, Massachusetts, Montana, Nebraska, New Jersey, New Mexico, and North Carolina. Project workers have the opportunity of deriving considerable knowledge and practical experience in the manipulating of wood-turning machines, the use of hand tools, the mixing and application of paints, and other skills connected with production of this type.

Library projects.—Considerable interest attaches to the participation of National Youth Administration youth on library projects. On the basis of figures submitted by the majority of State youth directors during the months of March, April, and June 1937 it is estimated that 5 percent of the employees on youth work projects were performing various types of library work.

The library work carried on by the National Youth Administration through its work program includes such activities as clerical assistance, bookkeeping, and page service; the establishment of branch libraries and new libraries in communities lacking such facilities; the establishment of traveling libraries; and bookbinding and repair work for schools and locally supported libraries and colleges.[29]

Construction projects.—A minor construction program was initiated by the National Youth Administration in December 1936, since which time this type of project has rapidly expanded in almost every State. The National Youth Administration construction program has been planned from the educational and cultural point of view to provide facilities for recreational purposes and for the benefit of the community at large.

As a result of this program, thousands of youth have been employed on small construction projects of the following kinds: Small rural schoolhouses, annexes to public buildings and schools, field houses, cooperative dormitories, county garages, bus shelters along highways, small bridges, cabins and shelter houses in parks, and community houses for recreational purposes.

In Oklahoma, for example, the State youth administration in cooperation with several public agencies has concentrated on a State-wide construction program which employs about 500 or 600 youth each month in the erection of small buildings. For the most part, these buildings are made of native stone, old brick, and other salvaged materials. At Shawnee a work center is being built in connection with the school system. The building is constructed of used paving brick donated by the city, and when completed will provide facilities for practical work in homemaking, shop work, and gardening, which the public school system will finance.

At Wetumka, Oklahoma, youth are constructing on the high school grounds two buildings of hollow tile and brick with a stone veneer. One is a homemaking building for girls, and the other is a boys' workshop. The project also includes

---

[29] See Carleton B. Joeckel, Library Service, The Advisory Committee on Education, Staff Study No. 11 (Washington: U. S. Government Printing Office, 1938), p. 55, for favorable comment on the contribution of the NYA in the field of library service.

the construction of tennis courts and gardens. The city school system will assume the responsibility of financing the operation of the buildings after they are completed.

An evaluation of construction projects.—During the summer of 1937, at the request of the National Youth Administration, a careful and thorough survey involving the use of a score card was made by the engineering division of the Works Progress Administration for the rating of 108 construction projects administered by the National Youth Administration.[30] In view of the importance of construction projects in the work projects program, the significance of such a report can well be appreciated. There is every reason for crediting the investigators with impartiality as well as with an understanding of the more fundamental problems of youth in economic society.

In general, the findings of the survey are favorable; the construction program as a whole is rated "very good." Most of the projects are of value to the public, and popular acceptance has provided adequate guarantees that they will be maintained after completion. "The projects are almost universally well located." Although some of the economies practiced and the occasional inappropriate use of material "do not warrant general commendation," the planning of the projects in relation to community needs and from the aesthetic point of view is acceptably satisfactory. "The public value of the . . . work is generally excellent."

From the point of view of the youth employed, the educational value of the projects in general is rated "good." But the surveyors deplore those projects in which the activities of the workers are limited to simple manual operations, or in which little or no effort is made to stimulate youthful initiative and to encourage the participation of the employees in the planning of the work. In this connection, apparently, almost everything depends upon the character of the foreman or the supervisor. Instances of

---

[30] WPA interoffice memorandum, September 22, 1937. Credit for the compilation of this memorandum is due to Perry A. Fellows, of the WPA engineering division. The score card items relating to the evaluation of educational and supervisory aspects of the projects were prepared by Palmer O. Johnson, of the Advisory Committee on Education.

excellent leadership and job training on various projects are reported. In general the projects seem to have aroused the interest of the youth employed, though in varying degree, and the surveyors note considerable improvement in social attitudes.

The surveyors were asked to evaluate the correlation of the job with supplementary school work or special training. They reported that "usually the construction projects have little or nothing to offer in this respect." Nevertheless they agreed that the disciplinary value of work is in itself of educational significance; even if it be only to learn "what an hour's work means" the youth "could hardly miss learning something useful."

There is little marked evidence that the projects serve to displace adult workers or to increase the local supply of nonrelief labor; and the funds undoubtedly have been applied to advantage, as intended, in the employment of relief labor. On the other hand, there is evidence in several instances of "failure to secure the cooperation of organized labor."

The health of the youth and the safety conditions under which they work are satisfactory. Projects are operated in an orderly fashion, and the equipment is properly cared for.

Educational Provision for Youth on Work Projects

In discussing educational provision for youth on work projects it is important to recognize the distinction between the specific provision that is made for youth on work projects and the more general program for unemployed out-of-school youth as a group. The National Youth Administration, as part of its general policy, encourages any program for the education of unemployed out-of-school youth. It serves as a stimulating and even as an initiating and coordinating agency, but it is not a facilitating agency. It does not provide funds, teachers, or equipment. Facilitation is properly the function of existing educational agencies, Federal, State, and local.

The National Youth Administration is especially desirous, however, of improving the educational experience of young people employed on youth work projects, and to effect this end stimulates both the youth and the local educational agencies. Although it cannot compel employees to attend classes, it can inform them of available classes; advise which will be most useful; encourage them to attend classes and give them special opportunities to attend; and even exert negative pressures by indicating that the National Youth Administration is not prepared to help those who are not willing to improve themselves educationally. On the other hand, it can encourage local educational agencies to establish classes which will be useful to youth employed on projects and to provide instruction free to those youth; have teachers visit the projects and give instruction there during or immediately after working hours; and employ foremen who in themselves are teachers and who give instruction to the youth on the job. To this extent the Youth Administration's interest in the education of project youth coincides with that of the educators' general program of education for youth out of school.

The Youth Administration has no definite national policy for the education of work projects youth. Determination of policy is left to local requirements, facilities, and initiative. Undoubtedly some of the most valuable trade training is given on the job itself. That fact, however, should not be allowed to distract attention from the essential question as to what related occupational training should deliberately be given to youth employed on work projects.

The evidence available at the national office is limited to reports from State youth directors, and those reports are not, generally speaking, specific and pertinent to the issue of education of work projects youth. They describe what is being done in educating out-of-school youth as a whole—for example, reports [31] of June 1937 from 40 States estimate that only about one-fifth of all unemployed out-of-school youth are receiving formal continuation schooling of any

---

[31] In reply to a telegram from the NYA to State youth directors, June 28, 1937, in relation to a joint inquiry with the American Youth Commission. Replies in the files of the NYA.

sort—but they seldom state such items as the number of project youth who are attending classes, by whom the classes are administered, what the courses of instruction are, when they are given, what facilities are provided to enable project youth to attend classes, what value such classes have been to project youth, how the classes have affected their work, and whether the teacher also is employed as foreman on the project itself. Indeed, the usual impression gained from a reading of the reports of State youth directors is that too often the education of work projects youth is a sporadic development, depending primarily on local interest or the endeavor of some individual, and is in general simply an incidental issue in the larger program of education for out-of-school youth.

Where provision is made for the continued education of youth employed on work projects, the principal kinds are as follows: Special courses established at trade schools; courses in opportunity schools; class work under the auspices of State education departments; emergency education classes under the Works Progress Administration; and general and vocational class work in schools, colleges, and universities.

The following descriptions are examples, taken at random, of what is being done to educate project youth in various States. They are taken from the reports of State youth directors as of June 1937.[32]

In Connecticut it was estimated that over 200 project youth were attending vocational and general classes.

In Georgia 1,861 project youth were attending Works Progress Administration emergency education classes.

In Decatur, Illinois, it was reported that "every youth on a project attends a course of his choice unless excused for cause."

In Indiana emergency education teachers of the Works Progress Administration had given instruction to about 200 National Youth Administration youth in filing, shorthand, and other business practices, as well as art instruction, stagecraft, and household training.

In Kentucky approximately 2,000 National Youth Administration workers had participated in organized classes in

[32] In the files of the NYA.

such subjects as first aid, child care, bricklaying, weaving, and stone masonry.

In Mississippi the Works Progress Administration education division had enrolled 450 National Youth Administration youth in homemaking classes and 800 in domestic service classes.

In the State of Washington 618 work projects youth were enrolled in Works Progress Administration education division classes.

A project at the State Agricultural and Mechanical Institute in Alabama employed 20 boys who work at beautifying the campus and also attend trade courses at the institution. At the University of Alabama a similar arrangement allowed 36 rural girls to attend classes in home economics while working on a youth work project sponsored by the institution. A public trades school cosponsored a project enabling 40 project youth to attend the school while at work.

Almost two-thirds of the youth on work projects in New Mexico were attending after-work classes in general and vocational subjects.

Cooperating with the Prairie View State Normal and Industrial College for Negroes, the Texas Youth Administration had established a work project for Negro girls. Groups of 50 girls worked on this project for 12 weeks, lived in the dormitory, and attended domestic training classes.

In Lucas County, Ohio, during December 1937, about 500 out of 600 youth on work projects were attending classes, at an average attendance rate of 85 percent.

In Arkansas over 800 project youth attended part-time classes conducted by vocational teachers.

The resident agricultural projects referred to elsewhere in this chapter represent an outstanding illustration of some of the most interesting and significant work that is being done in connection with the continued education of work projects youth.

Although specific information covering a sufficiently comprehensive survey of current accomplishments is not available, it would appear that, despite the lack of a definite program, many youth engaged on work projects are attending classes and continuing their education. In some cases attendance is purely voluntary; in others the youths are subject to varying degree of "encouragement to attend" by supervising officials. On many projects the only form of training—and, insofar as the foremen are competent instructors, an undeniably excellent one—is that given by foremen on the jobs themselves. Apparently, however, the public schools and the emergency education division of the Works Progress Administration bear the major part of the load of formal education. But some of the most interesting and significant achievements are those in which an educational agency, such as a vocational school or a college, has extended its educational facilities to youth employed on youth work projects sponsored by the agency concerned. The possibilities of further development in this connection should not be overlooked.

An interesting and illuminating comment on the attitude of Youth Administration employees toward classes for work project youth is presented in the following excerpts from a communication of the Ohio State youth director.

At the start of the educational program for all youth on NYA, there was evidence of some resentment on the part of nearly half of the group. The teachers are, however, apparently very successful in overcoming this attitude, particularly among the girls and among the boys above tenth grade educational level. Some apathy does exist among the boys in the lower educational group. They present the one problem that now faces the educational program. This group of boys has a dislike of anything which is not of a very practical, routine nature. They are the type of boys who can go into any factory and spend the rest of their lives doing a highly repetitive operation, hour after hour, day after day, and be happy on the job. They do practically no reading, except that which is limited to certain sections of newspapers and cheap magazines. The problem seems to be one of the overcoming this innate attitude of inertia, even more than the problem of overcoming any resentment toward an educational program as part of the work program.

It would be remembered that even in our formal system of education, every classroom has some youth who do not adjust to the standardized curricula. That these youth are a problem to their supposedly highly trained educators, cannot be denied. To have a whole classroom of such persons presents a real teaching problem. The teachers are, however, rapidly learning to talk on the educational level of the group they are teaching and are improving in their ability to make the work practical and interesting to a group who find it difficult to learn. * * *

While during the first few weeks of the program there was some skepticism—and the outlook seemed discouraging—it is now generally the feeling on the part of the instructors and youth that the educational program is proving very worthwhile and beneficial. * * *[33]

Probably the most significant of all illustrations of a program for the continued education of work project youth is that provided at Passamaquoddy Village in Maine, where the National Youth Administration has established a work and training project for male youth on relief rolls in New England. The boys are proposed as candidates by specially appointed local committees, but are finally selected, on a quota basis, primarily in terms of their need for varied experiences from which to choose an occupation. From June 1 to October 31, 1937, a group of approximately 250 boys was enrolled at Quoddy.[34] For the second course, in progress from January 15, 1938, about 150 boys were enrolled.[35]

The boys are engaged in maintenance work on the buildings constructed at the time that the Quoddy tidal-power project was contemplated. As many as 25 different kinds of occupational activity are called for. Each boy selects three occupations in which he is interested, and works for about 6 weeks at each. He receives $20 a month, plus subsistence and medical care. Half of each day, Monday through Friday, is spent on job work in the shops or on the grounds; the other half is spent in the classroom studying related subjects. Much practical instruction is given on the job.

At the expiration of his training period the boy is returned to his home with a copy of his record while at camp. In many instances these records have helped the local committee, which initially proposed him, to place the boy in private employment. His experience, although it has not trained him specifically for a job, has been of practical value, and gives him an advantage over other applicants for jobs; he has a definite idea of the sort of work he will have to do if he is employed on a job of a type he tried out at Quoddy; he has developed good working habits; and his morale has been restored.

[33] Communication to the national office, January 17, 1938. In the files of the NYA.
[34] National Youth Administration Work Experience Project, Quoddy Village, Maine. Composite Progress Report, June–October 1937. Mimeographed.
[35] WPA News Release 6-249, February 8, 1938, p. 10.

Concluding Statement

The work projects program has provided work experience to thousands of youth who otherwise might have remained unemployed and idle for years or who, if employed, might have proved of little value or even temporarily a liability to their first employers. At the same time it has helped to supplement the income of relief families.

To the extent that projects have been well planned, with due recognition of educational values, and executed under the sympathetic guidance of informed supervisors, it is probably true that many youth have gained valuable educational and work experience. Because of their tendency to emphasize production at the expense of the youthful employee, and because of the low caliber of their supervisory and technical personnel, some projects are not altogether creditable; but such projects of poor quality are in the minority. The considerable majority of projects, have been well planned and, in general, have been decidedly beneficial in improving the social attitudes of young people. They have probably helped to reduce the amount of juvenile delinquency.

The program has contributed to the improvement of local communities, and has demonstrated to those communities constructive ways of engaging out-of-school unemployed youth and improving their morale. The work projects, aided by Federal funds, have made possible the completion of many valuable social enterprises which otherwise could not have been attempted by local communities dependent entirely on their own resources. That the communities are aware of the value of these projects is evidenced by the extent to which local governmental agencies sponsor them. And as a result, the public has become more fully aware of the economic and educational problems of youth.

The policy of insisting on a local sponsor for every project has tended to reduce Federal costs and to stimulate local contributions, and simultaneously to awaken the interest of the local community in the problems of its youth.

The wide variety of experience available on the work projects program has resulted in several valuable experiments, among which resident agricultural training projects and the Quoddy training project promise to be the most fruitful from an educational and social point of view. The significant characteristics of these projects are: The objective, which provides a program combining work and education in related subjects; the sponsorship, which guarantees the youth employed a course of related training while on the job; and the social nature of the program, which calls for continuous residence at the site of the project over a definite period of several months. The possibilities of this type of program have not yet been fully explored, but already these projects have yielded suggestive experience of profound educational and social significance. Experimentation of this nature is appropriate as a Federal function; it should be encouraged as a cooperative enterprise between Federal and State agencies.

The student aid program has been widely approved by educators and the public at large. Perhaps that approval has been somewhat unduly affected by the dramatic values in the college aid aspects of the program, with the result that the possible inadequacies of the far more extensive school aid program are glossed over. But the value of the work projects program has not received its proportionate share of recognition. It is in many ways the more significant program and undoubtedly warrants careful consideration. It is particularly unfortunate, in this connection, that the information available on the characteristics of work project youth is, by comparison with that for student aid recipients, so inadequate and incomplete.

The work projects program employs only two-fifths as many youth as does the student aid program, but the age range of the youth group employed is narrower. Its annual allotment is one and one-half times as large, and in terms of total Federal cost per youth assisted it is three times as expensive. But this allotment, in contrast with that for the student aid program, is made on the basis of 12 rather than 9 months of the year, and includes the cost of supervision and materials. Whereas student aid is largely in the nature of educational maintenance, the wages received by more than 95 percent of work project employees are needed for strictly relief purposes. And, whereas in the student aid program the employment factor is ancillary to the educational, in the work projects program the reverse principle operates.

For youth employed on work projects the principal need is work experience. Prior to enlistment on the project one-third have had no work experience and most of the remainder have had only sketchy experience in unskilled and semiskilled occupations. Youth employed on work projects are given work experience of a practical and useful nature, as a result of which many are able to find and occupy jobs in private industry. The wide variety of work experience on the projects makes it possible to provide many of these young people with the specific work experience which they seek. And, apart from practical instruction on the job, workers are encouraged to attend continuation classes in related and general subjects so as to improve their educational qualifications. Nevertheless, although the educational byproducts have been substantial, much remains to be done before the work projects can be justified on this basis alone.

Although not all of the projects have been worth while, the experience of the National Youth Administration in its work projects program has in general been of value. Much depends on the quality of local supervision, which shows signs of much needed improvement. Experience has demonstrated the possibilities of an inexpensive program of work training for out-of-school youth, presumably sufficient to provide many of them with the experience necessary for admission to private employment. Second, it has shown that youth work projects can be initiated and conducted by local communities to the ultimate mutual benefit of the youth and the community. And, third, it has provided considerable evidence to justify the further development of a program of work combined with education of a practical nature for those youth to whom the conventional school curriculum is distasteful or ill adapted.

CHAPTER V
OTHER PROGRAMS

As part of its duties, the National Youth Administration has, at one time or another, taken over the financing and, to some extent, the administration of several programs other than those already discussed, namely: The vocational guidance and placement program; the apprentice training program; and the program of educational camps for unemployed women. The last-mentioned has been discontinued, and the apprentice training program has been transferred to the United States Department of Labor; but the guidance and placement program is still financed and directed by the National Youth Administration.

Vocational Guidance and Placement

The vocational guidance and placement program of the National Youth Administration is usually referred to as the Junior Placement Service. It is designed primarily to give vocational guidance and to provide placement service to the vast body of unemployed youth who are out of school. It is not limited to youth aided by the National Youth Administration in its major programs. The group eligible for registration, interviewing, counseling, and placement has been specified as all young people 16 to 21 years of age and all young people 21 to 24 years of age who are inexperienced.

The junior placement program was first put in operation in June 1936, in cooperation with the United States Employment Service. The National Youth Administration supplied a limited amount of funds to provide personnel to staff a junior division for young applicants within the Employment Service. It was anticipated that by this means the State employment services would become informed of the problems of youth placement and the methods of handling them, and that the States would eventually take over the junior division personnel on their own budgets. This expectation is already being fulfilled, for example, in Connecticut, Indiana, Kentucky, Massachusetts, North Carolina, Texas, and Wisconsin.[1] Other States have indicated their intention of taking over the junior divisions.

Junior counselors function as members of the Employment Service staff. They are approved jointly by the Director of the Division of Guidance and Placement of the National Youth Administration and by the Director of the United States Employment Service. The junior placement division is housed in quarters within or adjoining those of the State employment services.

The States have been allowed freedom, within the general framework of the national program, to develop means and methods for providing guidance and placement services in accordance with their specific needs. Because of the resultant variation in the number, type, and quality of the agencies, facilities, and services thus made available, the opportunity for cooperation on the part of the National Youth Administration has also varied. Cooperation has necessarily involved the preparation of material on occupational information for all youth; but the principal significance of the program, so far as the National Youth Administration is concerned, resides in its practical usefulness to youth employed on youth work projects.

The methods of operating the guidance and placement program most commonly in use are: (1) Conducting occupational classes; (2) preparing occupational pamphlets; (3) giving radio programs; (4) rendering individual counseling service through trained technical assistants; (5) compiling youth personnel records; (6) preparing directories of opportunities for training and recreation; (7) issuing guidance manuals; and (8) stimulating interest in guidance by providing supervisors of guidance on State administrative staffs.

---

[1] WPA News Release 6-249, February 8, 1938, pp. 11-12.

The following duties are assigned to the staffs of the Junior Placement Service in the various States:
1. Interviewing young people who apply for jobs.
2. Referring them to available jobs in private industry.
3. Placing eligible youth on work relief projects and following up their success on these projects as a basis for placement in private industry.
4. Referring eligible youth to apprentice-training committees and Civilian Conservation Corps recruiting bureaus.
5. Advising young people as to the desirability of returning to school, and providing them with full information about available educational institutions.
6. Referring youth eligible for National Youth Administration student aid to the proper awarding authorities.
7. Providing young people with information as to the available resources for training in the kind of work they are seeking.
8. Giving information about opportunities for leisure-time activities available in the community, and about available health agencies and clinics.
9. Cooperating with all local agencies, educational and social, which deal with young people of the youth age group.

For the period from June 1936 through December 1937 the total cost of the National Youth Administration guidance and placement program, included as part of the national administrative expenses, was $297,916. By the end of this period 77 junior placement offices had been established in 32 States and the District of Columbia.[2] Some of these have since been closed. A total of 65 were in operation in February 1938.

Of new applicants at these offices one-fifth (19 percent) have had no high school training, and almost one-half (46 percent) have graduated from high school; one-fourth (26 percent) are under 18 years of age and one-eighth (12 percent) are 21 years old or older; two-thirds (65 percent) have had previous work experience. A measure of the accomplishments of the program is provided in the statistics relating to the 18-month period ending December 1937. During this period over 190,000 youth registered with the junior placement offices and almost 100,000 placements were made, of which more than nine-tenths (93,771) were in

[2] Ibid.

private employment.[3] It is evident from these statistics that junior placement offices have not been devoting a major share of their attention to placement of youth on emergency projects.

Apprentice Training [4]

The Federal Committee on Apprentice Training was created by Executive Order No. 6750–C on June 27, 1934, for the purpose of maintaining an apprentice training program under the National Recovery Administration codes. It was administered by the United States Department of Labor with funds provided by the National Recovery Administration. When the National Industrial Recovery Act was declared unconstitutional, the Committee's functions were transferred by the President on August 11, 1935, to the National Youth Administration, which had already been assigned as one of its functions the promotion of apprenticeship. Supervision by the National Youth Administration under this arrangement remained nominal. The Committee continued to operate from offices in the Department of Labor but with the full cooperation of the Youth Administration, which provided the funds and was also represented on the Committee. By Federal statute,[5] in August 1937, the functions of the Committee were transferred to the Department of Labor. At that time the funds that had been provided by the National Youth Administration for the purposes of this Committee totaled approximately $119,000.[6]

Educational Camps for Unemployed Women

The program of educational camps for unemployed women was established in the summer of 1934 under the direction of the Division of Education Projects of the Federal Em-

---

[3] Data supplied by the NYA.
[4] A more detailed discussion of this program is presented in a report by John Dale Russell and associates, Vocational Education, The Advisory Committee on Education, Staff Study No. 8 (Washington: U. S. Government Printing Office, 1938).
[5] Public, No. 308, 75th Cong., 1st sess. (August 16, 1937).
[6] Information supplied by the NYA.

ergency Relief Administration.[7] The camps were intended primarily for women who had lost their jobs and were in need of personal and occupational rehabilitation. Among the chief features of the camp life were recreational activities, self-government, cooperative living, personal guidance, and the study of problems of interest to women workers in industry. The training period lasted from 1 to 4 months.

During the fiscal year 1934–35 enrollments totaled 1,840 in 28 camps in 27 States. During the following year, 1935–36, State directors for the National Youth Administration were authorized to organize the camps, which, however, were supervised by the Division of Education Projects of the Federal Emergency Relief Administration, which also provided the funds. During the first half of this year enrollments rose to 3,112 in 47 camps in 27 States. But funds ran short. During the period January through June 1936, enrollments dropped to 2,345 in 15 camps in only 11 States.[8]

In July 1936, for purposes of administrative convenience, the entire program was transferred to the National Youth Administration [9] as an official work project for which special funds were provided.[10] The complexion of the program now inevitably changed. Under the new auspices the program, instituted primarily for older women temporarily unemployed, became one principally for female youth, most of whom, by virtue of age, never had been employed. The new program provided elementary training in self-expression, health education, and home economics. Group recreation constituted a major activity. The girls received individual counseling. A certain amount of workers' education persisted. The girls worked at relatively simple jobs, such as book repairing and the preparation of certain hospital and household supplies. From October 1936 to June 1937 enrollments totaled approximately 3,500 in 29 camps in 22 States.[11]

[7] FERA Communication E-24, May 23, 1934.
[8] Data from tables supplied by the NYA.
[9] Presidential Letter No. 5064 (July 13, 1936).
[10] See p. 17, footnote 16.
[11] Typewritten report of the Director of Educational Camps for Unemployed Women to the Deputy Executive Director of the NYA, August 12, 1937, p. 55. A supplement covers the period July 1 to October 1, 1937. Both reports are in files of the NYA.

With the commencement of the fiscal year 1937–38 the question arose as to the desirability of continuing the camp program.[12] The available evidence on costs per enrollee was ambiguous and varied considerably from camp to camp; it appeared that, possibly because of the fact that every camp operated as a project in itself, the average cost was at least $30 and in some cases as high as $45. Although undoubtedly less than the corresponding figure for boys in the Civilian Conservation Corps, with which, by a misleading analogy, the women's camps were often compared, this average was somewhat higher than that for youth on work projects. Furthermore, because women enrolled in these camps were not provided with the cost of transportation to the camp or with a relief wage which they might send home to their families as a partial substitute for their own services, some difficulty was experienced in persuading women to enroll. It is also probable that parents objected to having their daughters leave home to go to resident camps.

Consequently, despite the fact that some of the State youth directors strongly represented the point of view of their advisory committees as favoring the general idea of educational camps for women and girls, it was decided to abandon the program, and in October it was terminated. The reason for this decision is in part attributable to the development of a new kind of program. A few months before it was finally decided to abandon the women's camp, the program of resident agricultural camps for youth on work projects had been initiated and gave promise of immediate success. These camps were found to be only a little more expensive than the regular work projects, but still noticeably less costly than the educational camps for women for which as a substitute they proved adequate in many respects. Consequently the final abandonment of the old program did not constitute a complete loss, although some of the best characteristics of that program, namely, self-government, cooperative management, personal guidance, and workers' education were now relegated to a less important role.

---

[12] During the period July through September 1937 enrollments dropped to approximately 1,500 in 16 camps in 15 States.

Women's camps as originally conceived are obviously not appropriate to the present youth program. If ever they should be resuscitated in the form of the venture in its earlier stages, it would seem advisable that they should be made part of an adult program.

CHAPTER VI

EVALUATION OF THE CONTRIBUTIONS OF THE NATIONAL YOUTH ADMINISTRATION

The various programs of the National Youth Administration have been discussed in some detail in the preceding chapters of this study. In this chapter an effort will be made to evaluate the contributions of the youth administration and its programs to (1) the solution of the relief problem; (2) the establishment, development, and extension of educational concepts and policies; (3) the solution of urgent problems of youth; (4) cooperative activity in local communities; and (5) Federal administrative policy.

The Relief Problem

Adequate statistics from which to determine the extent to which the National Youth Administration has contributed to the solution of the relief problem are not available. Only a rough estimate is possible. Of all persons registered in the unemployment census of November 1937, approximately 1,100,000 persons 16 to 19 years of age and about 1,300,000 persons 20 to 24 years of age were reported as either "totally unemployed" (but not necessarily on relief) or employed as "emergency workers" (necessarily on relief). "Emergency workers" alone constituted about one-fifth of the total within the age group 15 to 24.[1] If it may be assumed that of the 15 to 19 year age group reported in the unemployment census roughly two-thirds are 18 to 19 years of age,[2] it may be estimated that there were approximately 2,000,000 persons 18 to 24 years of age in the "totally unemployed or employed on emergency work" category, of whom approximately 400,000 were in "emergency work."

---
[1] Estimated from data supplied by the Census of Partial Employment, Unemployment, and Occupations. See p. 3, footnote 4.
[2] Analysis of school attendance data from the 1930 census provides a basis for this assumption.

But in that same month, November 1937, the National Youth Administration employed approximately 122,000 youth aged 18 to 24 on (emergency) work projects. It thus provided for at least one-twentieth of all youth aged 18 to 24 who were totally unemployed or on emergency work, and about one-fourth of those on emergency (relief) work.

To what extent beyond the conservative measure here determined it is reasonable to go by the inclusion of youth aided on the student aid program it is impossible to estimate. Relief is not the only criterion of eligibility for student aid as it is for employment on work projects. It is obvious, however, that the estimates of the proportion of unemployed youth aided by the National Youth Administration are definitely conservative.

In view of the fact that the hourly wages of youth employed on the work projects are directly proportional to those paid to adult workers on the works program, and that the latter in turn are determined in accord with prevailing standard rates for employment in private industry, it not infrequently happens that work project youth receive hourly wages higher than the average available locally to youth in private industry.[3] To this extent the National Youth Administration operates in conformity with the established Federal principle of security wage employment.

By adhering to accepted desirable policies relating to the minimum age for the participation of youth in gainful employment, it is probable that the National Youth Administration has helped to raise the level of wages and to lengthen the period of formal educational experience. By employing youth on public projects, the youth administration has helped to reduce pressure on the labor market and competition for jobs among adult workers. At the same time, it has provided youth with guidance, experience, and training against the time that they will join the ranks of adult applicants for employment.

---

[3] It should be noted, however, that youth employed on youth work projects are employed only on a part-time basis and at a maximum wage of $25 per month.

Educational Concepts and Policies

As an emergency agency, flexible in its administration and with relatively large available funds, the National Youth Administration has been able to experiment in educational programs which, under ordinary circumstances, would have received little consideration by regular agencies of Government, and which even today are not fully recognized by the majority of educators.

Through the extension of educational opportunities to the underprivileged, the Youth Administration has uncovered a reservoir of competent youth desirous of continued education for whom almost no provision has been made in the past. It has demonstrated the possibility of providing educational opportunities at small cost which have proved of considerable advantage to the youth and to the institutions involved. And, by providing merely the essentials for the maintenance of youth, it has increased school and college enrollments by 300,000 to 400,000 without sacrificing quality to quantity.

Experimentation which grew out of the necessity for combining work with schooling has demonstrated possibilities of profound educational significance. Especially noteworthy in this connection are those work projects, sponsored by educational institutions, in which youth are maintained in residence at the institutions and undergo a course of training related to their employment on work of benefit to the institutions themselves. To the extent that the National Youth Administration has been successful in thus combining work and schooling, the more pointedly by contrast does it emphasize the inadequacies of the conventional current curriculum and guidance policies at both high school and college levels.

Although the nominal aim of the National Youth Administration has been to serve as a relief agency, it has actually fulfilled an educational function as well. Because relief was the primary objective, the educational policy of the Youth Administration has of necessity been of a temporizing and exigent nature. Had the educational function been considered as of primary rather than of secondary importance, it is not unlikely that the policies and programs here reported would have been considerably altered. To the conflicting practices inevitably resultant from this confusion concerning the relative importance of the functions of relief and education may in large measure be attributed many of the apparent discrepancies and inconsistencies in the present program.

Urgent Problems of Youth

If there is today a "lost generation" of youth lacking work experience, lacking guidance, abandoned by the school, and disowned by industry, and if, as is often claimed, the new social and economic status of youth resultant from changes in the age composition of the population calls for national leadership in meeting the problems of youth, then it must be conceded that in large measure the National Youth Administration has contributed significantly toward the solution of these problems.

Without doubt the depression adversely affected the morale of youth. But by providing youth with an articulate agency for the expression of their needs and a focal point of direct action in meeting them, the National Youth Administration has helped to restore their morale. The indictment that actual achievement has failed to measure up to the demand for service becomes, therefore, a criticism not of inadequacy in function so much as of limitations in application. Through each of its major programs the National Youth Administration has provided youth with facilities for continued education, work experience, practical guidance, and, so far as possible, placement in employment in private industry. There is much to indicate that the morale and health of youth participating in student aid and work projects employment have improved.

By experimenting with youth of unrevealed potentialities in unusual situations, the National Youth Administration has drawn attention to many inadequacies in the current provisions for vocational guidance. Many unemployed youth, poorly educated and untrained, are to all appearances fit for nothing but unskilled or semiskilled work; nevertheless, time and again, reports are received concerning the surprising extent of their achievements when given the right environment, an encouraging and skillful supervisor or foreman, and the chance to do constructive work.

Benefits to Local Communities

Liberal funds and a definite program have made it possible for the National Youth Administration to draw together in effective cooperation the frequently dissident and often individually impotent local agencies which exist in many communities. Under the leadership of the National Youth Administration and its advisory committees, of which these agencies are now constituent members, many communities have learned the advantage of united effort. It is not unreasonable to assume that some of the progress thus achieved will endure. Nor is the achievement limited to local communities. The coordination of interested agencies, both public and private, has been of such a nature that it may well be said that the youth program of today is limited to no geographical or political boundaries but is a part of the national life.

In demonstrating what concerted action can accomplish on behalf of youth the National Youth Administration has convinced many local communities that it is possible for them to employ, train, and direct their youth, and that, given proper direction and wise planning, the contributions made by the youth thus engaged are often of real and lasting value. In several instances, at their own expense, communities have taken over the responsibility and administration of programs initiated by the National Youth Administration.

Federal Administrative Policy

The National Youth Administration has cooperated successfully with private as well as public agencies, in groups and individually. Its success in conducting a Nation-wide enterprise through a system of decentralized control probably has had significant bearing on the relationship between Federal and State Governments in educational matters. By extending aid to individuals rather than to institutions or agencies it has avoided the implications of interference with the authority of local units. At the same time it has demonstrated not only that cooperative programs between agencies at different levels of control can be effective, but also that such programs offer possibilities of substantial economies in administration.

APPENDIX A

EXECUTIVE ORDER NO. 7086

Establishment of the National Youth Administration Within the Works Progress Administration

By virtue of and pursuant to the authority vested in me by the Emergency Relief Appropriation Act of 1935,[1] approved April 8, 1935 (Public Res. No. 11, 74th Cong.), I hereby establish the National Youth Administration, to be within the Works Progress Administration established under Executive Order No. 7034 of May 6, 1935.

There shall be a National Advisory Committee and an Executive Committee for the National Youth Administration. The members of said National Advisory Committee shall be representatives of labor, business, agriculture, education, and youth, to be appointed by the President. I hereby appoint Josephine Roche as chairman of said executive committee, to serve without additional compensation. The other members of said executive committee shall be appointed by the President.

The National Youth Administration shall be under the general supervision of the Administrator of the Works Progress Administration and under the immediate supervision of an executive director. I hereby appoint Aubrey W. Williams as executive director thereof, to serve without additional compensation. The said executive director shall also be a member of the Advisory Committee on Allotments, established under said Executive Order No. 7034 of May 6, 1935.

I hereby prescribe the following functions and duties of the National Youth Administration:

> To initiate and administer a program of approved projects which shall provide relief, work relief, and employment for persons between the ages of sixteen and twenty-five years who are no longer in regular attendance at a school requiring full time, and who are not regularly engaged in remunerative employment.

In the performance of such duties and functions, expenditures are hereby authorized for necessary supplies and equipment; law books, books of reference, directories, periodicals, newspapers, and press clippings; travel expenses, including the expense of attendance at meetings when specifically authorized by the executive director; and the executive director is hereby authorized to accept and utilize such voluntary and uncompensated services and, with the consent of the State, the

---

[1] The authority vested in the President has been continued by subsequent relief acts and the orders issued pursuant to it have remained in effect.

services of such State and local officers and employees, and appoint, without regard to the provisions of civil service laws, such officers and employees, as may be necessary, and prescribe the duties and responsibilities and, without regard to the Classification Act of 1923, as amended, fix the compensation of any officers and employees so appointed: *Provided*, That, in so far as practicable, the persons employed under the authority of this Executive order, shall be selected from those receiving relief.

Allocations will be made hereafter for administrative expenses and for authorized projects.

FRANKLIN D. ROOSEVELT

The WHITE HOUSE,
June 26, 1935.

EXECUTIVE ORDER NO. 7164

PRESCRIBING RULES AND REGULATIONS RELATING TO STUDENT-AID PROJECTS AND TO EMPLOYMENT OF YOUTH ON OTHER PROJECTS UNDER THE EMERGENCY RELIEF APPROPRIATION ACT OF 1935

REGULATION NO. 7

By virtue of and pursuant to the authority vested in me by the Emergency Relief Appropriation Act of 1935, approved April 8, 1935 (Public Resolution No. 11, 74th Congress), I hereby prescribe the following rules and regulations relating to student-aid projects and to employment of youth on other projects:

1.[2] *Definition of Student-Aid Projects.* Student-aid projects are hereby defined to be projects financed, in whole or in part, from funds appropriated by the Emergency Relief Appropriation Act of 1935, which provide financial assistance to needy young people in amounts which will permit them to continue their education in primary schools, high schools, colleges, or graduate schools, in exchange for part-time work upon useful projects.

2. *Supervision of Student-Aid Projects.* Student-aid projects shall be supervised by the National Youth Administration.

3.[2] *Amount of Aid.* Disbursement of student-aid funds shall conform to the following requirements:

(a) No primary-school or high-school student shall be paid more than $6 per month for the school year.

(b) No college student shall be paid more than $20 per month for the school year, and the average of all payments made to college students during the school year shall not exceed $15 per month per student.

---

[2] As revised by Executive Order No. 7319, March 18, 1936.

(c) No graduate student shall be paid more than $40 per month for the school year, and the average of all payments made to graduate students during the school year shall not exceed $30 per month per student.

4. *Administration of Student-Aid Projects.* Methods for the selection of eligible students to receive student aid, the character of the work to be performed by the recipients of student aid, and all conditions of employment shall be determined by, or under the direction of, the Executive Director of the National Youth Administration.

5.[3] *Employment of Youth on Projects.* The maximum and minimum hours of work, the conditions of employment and the monthly earnings to be paid young persons eligible for benefits under the National Youth Administration and employed on projects of the National Youth Administration (other than student-aid projects) and on projects of the Works Progress Administration shall be determined by the Works Progress Administration: Provided, however, that the monthly earnings applicable to part-time employment of such young persons shall not exceed fifty per centum (50%) of the schedule of monthly earnings as set forth in Executive Order No. 7046, dated May 20, 1935, and amendments thereto.

6. *Non-application of Regulations Nos. 1, 2, and 3.* The provisions of Regulation No. 1 as amended (Executive Orders Nos. 7046, 7117, and 7119 of May 20, July 29, and July 30, 1935, respectively), Regulation No. 2 as amended (Executive Orders Nos. 7060 and 7125 of June 5 and August 5, 1935, respectively), and Regulation No. 3 (Executive Order No. 7083 of June 24, 1935) shall not be applicable to student-aid projects as defined in paragraph 1 or to the employment of young persons under paragraph 5 above.

FRANKLIN D. ROOSEVELT

THE WHITE HOUSE,
    August 29, 1935.

---

[3] As revised by Executive Order No. 7433, August 18, 1936.

APPENDIX B

TABLE 1.—*Financial assistance extended to college and graduate students from institutional and NYA sources, by States, 1936–37* [1]

State	Total aid	NYA aid		Institutional aid [2]		Percent NYA aid was of total aid
		Amount	Number of students	Amount	Number of students	
United States	$54,658,780	$16,225,994	180,990	$38,432,786	331,775	29.69
Alabama	779,945	224,512	2,402	555,433	4,886	28.79
Arizona	207,451	68,937	720	138,514	1,151	33.23
Arkansas	479,891	171,548	2,232	308,343	3,472	35.75
California	3,187,345	1,061,953	12,684	2,125,392	19,263	33.32
Colorado	626,550	162,401	2,029	464,149	4,455	25.92
Connecticut	1,237,189	115,044	1,348	1,122,145	5,841	9.30
Delaware	23,987	13,041	170	10,946	252	54.37
Florida	527,104	132,192	1,237	394,912	2,287	25.08
Georgia	1,024,534	367,324	4,201	657,210	5,893	35.85
Idaho	200,226	70,056	1,038	130,170	1,422	34.99
Illinois	3,421,803	975,028	10,649	2,446,775	25,273	28.49
Indiana	1,548,503	381,901	4,681	1,166,602	10,358	24.66
Iowa	1,665,345	433,925	4,987	1,231,420	14,201	26.06
Kansas	1,090,947	428,581	4,547	662,366	8,037	39.29
Kentucky	855,401	338,598	4,003	516,803	6,248	39.58
Louisiana	932,833	238,647	2,763	694,186	5,775	25.58
Maine	202,457	71,803	907	130,654	1,489	35.47
Maryland	843,630	178,518	1,840	665,112	3,313	21.16
Massachusetts	1,730,732	407,618	4,943	1,323,114	8,272	23.55
Michigan	1,877,857	586,092	6,205	1,291,765	14,835	31.21
Minnesota	1,061,376	440,203	4,534	621,173	5,371	41.47
Mississippi	451,071	168,564	2,455	282,507	3,511	37.37
Missouri	1,518,108	546,130	5,347	971,978	8,372	35.97
Montana	245,415	102,947	1,488	142,468	1,674	41.95
Nebraska	692,978	268,536	2,874	424,442	4,699	38.75
Nevada	23,434	11,818	176	11,616	249	50.43
New Hampshire	389,442	51,625	759	337,817	2,354	13.26
New Jersey	679,128	199,680	2,435	479,448	3,543	29.40
New Mexico	134,834	43,787	494	91,047	1,017	32.47
New York State	2,794,807	555,718	6,123	2,239,089	13,725	19.88
New York City	2,940,070	1,209,977	10,103	1,730,093	7,984	41.15
North Carolina	1,466,363	453,779	4,927	1,012,584	10,338	30.95
North Dakota	283,220	154,218	1,592	129,002	1,538	54.45
Ohio	2,828,106	765,721	7,688	2,062,385	18,134	27.08
Oklahoma	1,037,637	566,318	6,267	471,319	5,990	54.58
Oregon	645,239	152,434	2,135	492,805	5,525	23.62
Pennsylvania	4,250,603	915,127	10,887	3,335,476	20,763	21.53
Rhode Island	336,106	75,741	805	260,365	1,590	22.53
South Carolina	507,449	234,760	2,826	272,689	3,264	46.26
South Dakota	417,070	125,346	1,337	291,724	2,761	30.05
Tennessee	1,329,639	355,244	3,899	974,395	8,524	26.72
Texas	2,827,140	846,210	9,114	1,980,930	18,542	29.93
Utah	402,644	142,413	3,267	260,231	3,394	35.37
Vermont	417,396	47,334	658	370,062	2,563	11.34
Virginia	1,420,938	287,007	3,026	1,133,931	9,172	20.20
Washington	868,799	265,982	2,944	602,817	7,113	30.61
West Virginia	373,832	168,099	1,925	205,733	2,158	44.97
Wisconsin	994,064	430,655	4,955	563,409	7,091	43.32
Wyoming	147,484	32,486	620	114,998	1,607	22.03
District of Columbia	671,420	167,784	1,450	503,636	2,140	24.99
Puerto Rico	39,238	12,632	294	26,606	346	32.19

[1] Institutional aid as of 1936–37 reported during the summer of 1937 in support of requests for aid on 1937–38 program. Data supplied by the NYA.
[2] From affidavits submitted by institutions participating in the college and graduate aid programs. Institutional aid includes scholarships, fellowships, grants-in-aid, loans to students, and amounts expended as regular operations.

TABLE 2.—*Quota allotments and applications for student aid, by States and by type of aid, 1936-37* [1]

State	School aid [2]		College aid [3]		Graduate aid [4]	
	Quota	Applicants	Quota	Applicants	Quota	Applicants
United States	242,771	371,673	119,219	216,546	5,726	6,942
Alabama	3,153	4,908	1,687	4,068	17	28
Arizona	971	1,457	508	[5] 1,746	10	14
Arkansas	3,939	([6])	881	([6])	3	([6])
California	7,401	8,817	8,208	([6])	381	([6])
Colorado	3,713	4,620	1,195	1,642	68	37
Connecticut	1,756	2,289	533	[5] 1,112	265	300
Delaware	195	([6])	99	145	([6])	([6])
Florida	2,973	5,946	991	3,215	9	9
Georgia	6,068	9,586	2,823	6,889	115	[5] 152
Idaho	1,285	2,086	608	1,667	11	21
Illinois	14,284	15,707	6,969	[5] 13,170	754	682
Indiana	6,204	7,215	2,715	6,496	104	125
Iowa	3,372	3,862	2,501	4,019	164	197
Kansas	5,828	9,931	3,210	3,914	106	85
Kentucky	9,195	9,508	2,297	[5] 2,812	33	33
Louisiana	2,287	2,546	1,829	2,311	35	35
Maine	1,018	1,215	633	1,145	5	13
Maryland	1,655	1,909	1,256	1,611	75	84
Massachusetts	6,469	7,618	3,168	5,461	246	611
Michigan	9,458	13,441	4,240	8,916	231	435
Minnesota	5,395	6,541	3,295	3,822	97	47
Mississippi	2,274	12,220	1,273	5,769	5	7
Missouri	7,881	10,085	4,314	([6])	138	[5] 83
Montana	2,686	3,496	796	1,347	7	12
Nebraska	3,251	5,687	2,054	3,924	49	47
Nevada	145	218	96	202	1	1
New Hampshire	642	95	460	673	10	([5])
New Jersey	6,122	7,856	1,692	3,885	38	26
New Mexico	1,203	2,447	317	1,771	3	6
New York State	8,332	9,868	4,137	4,750	195	124
New York City	10,500	13,890	7,286	[5] 12,553	1,005	1,704
North Carolina	3,911	6,590	3,368	8,274	66	([6])
North Dakota	3,800	6,595	1,148	3,070	16	17
Ohio	11,851	18,112	5,364	[5] 13,412	207	408
Oklahoma	11,259	20,794	4,244	14,347	40	58
Oregon	1,054	1,970	1,126	2,858	21	26
Pennsylvania	20,940	49,803	6,914	([6])	245	([6])
Rhode Island	833	1,018	547	1,113	23	47
South Carolina	7,064	8,399	1,746	5,563	5	13
South Dakota	5,230	9,001	1,178	3,144	5	7
Tennessee	5,288	7,519	2,447	[5] 6,613	150	[5] 208
Texas	10,220	22,200	6,400	26,360	102	[5] 195
Utah	1,337	3,892	1,043	3,549	14	44
Vermont	392	631	362	914	10	7
Virginia	3,310	3,447	2,140	[5] 2,632	46	58
Washington	2,749	5,542	1,943	3,431	35	105
West Virginia	4,914	8,634	1,204	3,087	14	19
Wisconsin	8,137	11,083	4,159	[5] 7,336	346	494
Wyoming	417	799	392	609	4	4
District of Columbia	410	580	1,206	976	177	294
Alaska			17	20		
Hawaii			200	203	20	20

[1] Data compiled by the NYA from replies to NYA Circular Y-40 (November 25, 1936), 2 pp. Mimeographed.
[2] February 1937 quotas for 25,618 schools.
[3] November 1936 quotas for 1,656 institutions, applicants reported by 1,371 institutions.
[4] November 1936 quotas for 205 institutions, applicants reported by 160 institutions.
[5] Not all institutions reporting.
[6] Not reported.

APPENDIX B 97

TABLE 3.—*Recipients of college and graduate aid attending college in States other than State of legal residence, 1936–37* [1]

State	Total recipients, April 1937	Out-of-State residents receiving aid during 1936–37	Percent out-of-State recipients are of total
United States	138,882 [2]	21,430	15.4
Alabama	2,020	215	10.6
Arizona	566	58	10.2
Arkansas	1,524	(3)	(3)
California	8,599	(3)	(3)
Colorado	1,545	(3)	(3)
Connecticut	851	340	40.0
Delaware	125	(3)	(3)
Florida	1,125	96	8.5
Georgia	3,777	687	18.2
Idaho	764	128	16.8
Illinois	7,628	1,369	17.9
Indiana	3,746	1,038	27.7
Iowa	3,606	793	22.0
Kansas	3,808	495	13.0
Kentucky	3,403	419	12.3
Louisiana	2,337	190	8.1
Maine	765	173	22.6
Maryland	1,496	432	28.9
Massachusetts	3,465	1,027	29.6
Michigan	4,822	1,285	26.6
Minnesota	3,566	592	16.6
Mississippi	2,156	103	4.8
Missouri	4,562	1,001	22.0
Montana	1,032	62	6.0
Nebraska	2,290	351	15.3
Nevada	89 [4]	4	4.5
New Hampshire	533	113	21.2
New Jersey	2,068	231	11.2
New Mexico	461	31	6.7
New York [5]	12,779	1,668	13.1
North Carolina	3,970	1,060	26.7
North Dakota	1,478	85	5.8
Ohio	6,310	1,204	19.1
Oklahoma	4,964	332	6.7
Oregon	1,549	(4)	(4)
Pennsylvania	7,772	1,141	14.7
Rhode Island	631	219	34.7
South Carolina	2,161	351	16.2
South Dakota	1,140	67	5.9
Tennessee	2,975	1,228	41.3
Texas	7,274	(4)	(4)
Utah	1,844	240	13.0
Vermont	465	148	31.8
Virginia	2,420	893	36.9
Washington	2,141	125	5.8
West Virginia	1,552	171	11.0
Wisconsin	3,279	472	14.4
Wyoming	400	45	11.3
District of Columbia	1,049	748	71.3

[1] Summary of information received by the NYA from State youth directors in reply to oral and written requests from national office during summer of 1937.
[2] Total includes 89 for Nevada as of May 1937.
[3] Not reported.
[4] As of May 1937.
[5] Including New York City.

TABLE 4.—*Distribution of out-of-State college aid students by region of legal residence and region in which attending college, 1936–37* [1]

Region in which resident	Total resident in region	Region in which attending college					
		Northeast	Middle	Southeast	Northwest	Southwest	Far West
Total attending college in region	21,430	6,411	7,754	5,242	1,473	421	129
Northeast	8,963	5,062	2,225	1,552	101	20	3
Middle	5,475	623	3,598	620	559	64	11
Southeast	3,772	392	538	2,740	39	63	
Northwest	1,875	153	984	66	518	104	50
Southwest	778	76	194	220	139	149	
Far West	567	105	215	44	117	21	65

[1] Same source as appendix B table 3. Excluded from this table are Arkansas, California, Colorado, Delaware, Oregon, and Texas, which States failed to report. The States are grouped in regions according to the classification of the National Resources Committee, as follows: Northeast: Maine, New Hampshire, Vermont, Massachusetts, Rhode Island, Connecticut, New York, New Jersey, Delaware, Pennsylvania, Maryland, West Virginia, and the District of Columbia. Middle: Ohio, Indiana, Illinois, Michigan, Wisconsin, Minnesota, Iowa, and Missouri. Southeast: Virginia, North Carolina, South Carolina, Georgia, Florida, Kentucky, Tennessee, Alabama, Mississippi, Arkansas, and Louisiana. Northwest: North Dakota, South Dakota, Nebraska, Kansas, Montana, Idaho, Wyoming, Colorado, and Utah. Southwest: Oklahoma, Texas, New Mexico, and Arizona. Far West: Nevada, Washington, Oregon, California.

APPENDIX B

TABLE 5.—*Hours worked by, and earnings of, youth certified as on relief and employed on work projects operated by the National Youth Administration, by States, month ending May 31, 1937* [1]

State	Number of youth	Total hours worked	Total earnings	Average monthly earnings	Average hourly earnings
United States	175,538	7,459,631	$2,581,737	$14.71	$0.35
Alabama	3,977	191,844	45,569	11.46	.24
Arizona	544	21,773	7,358	13.58	.34
Arkansas	4,883	263,634	44,537	9.12	.17
California	5,769	210,119	99,626	17.27	.47
Colorado	1,648	68,905	22,696	13.77	.33
Connecticut	1,001	44,868	18,900	18.88	.42
Delaware	130	5,026	1,735	13.35	.35
Florida	2,409	124,945	28,420	11.80	.23
Georgia	4,763	213,285	47,742	10.02	.22
Idaho	1,011	40,379	16,009	15.83	.40
Illinois	9,410	396,517	167,475	17.80	.42
Indiana	3,182	113,635	50,554	15.89	.45
Iowa	1,017	38,956	14,821	14.57	.38
Kansas	4,446	167,664	53,378	12.01	.32
Kentucky	10,050	443,266	100,891	10.04	.23
Louisiana	3,385	149,307	42,379	12.52	.28
Maine	639	27,547	9,715	15.20	.35
Maryland	742	33,059	9,330	12.57	.28
Massachusetts	4,038	165,817	83,094	20.58	.50
Michigan	5,297	266,288	79,275	14.97	.30
Minnesota	3,599	144,306	59,713	16.59	.41
Mississippi	3,639	151,210	38,751	10.65	.26
Missouri	4,766	215,594	70,777	14.85	.33
Montana	927	33,405	15,884	17.13	.48
Nebraska	1,688	68,917	23,761	14.08	.35
Nevada	33	1,248	509	15.42	.41
New Hampshire	634	33,311	10,492	16.55	.32
New Jersey	4,475	178,198	84,012	18.77	.47
New Mexico	1,487	68,192	22,351	15.03	.33
New York State	8,448	315,069	154,910	18.34	.50
New York City	8,531	349,996	174,999	20.51	.49
North Carolina	3,105	163,897	35,532	11.44	.22
North Dakota	2,079	82,619	27,302	13.13	.33
Ohio	7,556	316,088	140,079	18.54	.44
Oklahoma	8,015	316,112	89,189	11.13	.28
Oregon	637	27,934	10,523	16.52	.38
Pennsylvania	14,336	495,632	260,204	18.15	.53
Rhode Island	553	24,979	9,800	17.72	.39
South Carolina	3,595	231,551	42,342	11.78	.18
South Dakota	2,978	124,240	38,297	12.86	.31
Tennessee	4,179	232,631	44,615	10.68	.19
Texas	7,652	324,174	81,226	10.62	.25
Utah	774	27,939	11,677	15.09	.42
Vermont	246	10,014	3,711	15.09	.37
Virginia	2,849	144,926	30,161	10.59	.21
Washington	1,608	59,088	27,535	17.12	.47
West Virginia	3,953	145,175	49,439	12.51	.34
Wisconsin	4,165	160,431	69,380	16.66	.43
Wyoming	293	12,038	4,703	16.05	.39
District of Columbia	397	13,883	6,338	15.96	.46

[1] Number of Youths and Adults Employed on Projects Operated by the National Youth Administration, by Relief Status and by States, Month Ending May 31, 1937, Works Progress Administration, Division of Research, Statistics and Records, NYA Series R-829 (July 2, 1937), tables 2-4, 10. Excludes 3,185 nonrelief youth.

APPENDIX C

TYPES OF COSPONSOR ON YOUTH WORK PROJECTS [1]

FEDERAL

Bureau of Entomology and Plant Quarantine, United States Department of Agriculture

STATE

Universities and colleges
Libraries
Library boards
University hospitals
College extension services
Departments of education
Departments of labor
Departments of public welfare
Departments of conservation

Attorneys general
Agricultural extension services
Agricultural experiment stations
Forestry services
Soil conservation services
Game, forestation, and parks commissions
Forest commissions
Planning boards

COUNTY

School boards
Superintendents of education
Training schools
Consolidated schools
Children's homes
Libraries
Boards of commissioners

Advisory boards or committees
Judges
Courts
Farm agents
Home demonstration clubs
Health departments
Road departments

CITY OR TOWNSHIP

School nurses
Schools
Opportunity schools
Boards of education
Parent-teacher associations
Adult education departments
Youth committees
Councils of social agencies
Relief agencies
Emergency bureaus
Planning commissions
Boards of supervisors
City commissions

Officers and departments
Councils
Mayors
City or town
Park boards
Recreation departments or commissions
Parks
Public libraries
Township road supervisors
Game farms
Chambers of commerce

[1] Compiled from replies to NYA Circular Y-45.

OTHER AGENCIES

Colleges and universities
Church asylums
Homes for crippled children
Medical research laboratories
Women's clubs
Junior women's clubs

Garden clubs
Lions clubs
Kiwanis clubs
American Legion posts
Civic organizations
Y. M. C. A.'s

APPENDIX D

TYPES OF WORK ACTIVITY IN WHICH YOUTH ENGAGE ON WORK PROJECTS [1]

Agriculture:
    Experimentation
    Testing
Artifacts excavated
Art work, maps and illustrations
Athletic courts constructed
Athletic instruction
Awnings made and installed
Baby cribs made and screened
Belts, bags, etc., sewed
Bicycle shed constructed
Bleachers built
Books, repair and care
Bricklaying
Bricks cleaned for reuse
Bridges, small, log, or stone, constructed
Bridle path constructed
Briefs on illegal law practices compiled
Broom-making
Building partitions dismantled
Buildings:
    Dismantled
    Frame, log, and stone constructed
    Remodeled
    Repaired
Cabinet work
Carpentry
Child care in homes
Classrooms, temporary, constructed
Class study coordinated with work projects
Cleaning, general household
Clerical work
Clothes, old, renovated
Clothing and costumes sewed
Concrete and mortar mixed and layed
Construction work:
    General
    Making of cement forms
    Granite columns
Cooking for homes, for lunchrooms, etc.
Curbs, signs, etc., painted
Curtains sewed
Dishwashing
Dolls and animals sewed
Domestic service (general)
Dormitories, temporary, constructed
Drafting
Driveways constructed
Fancywork made
Farm information on insects, weeds, etc., delivered
Farm land surveyed
Farm short course directory prepared
Farms mapped
Feeding game
Fences and walls constructed
Field data recorded
Filing and indexing public records, etc.
Fish and game conservation
Fish growth study from scales and length of fish
Flower and plant experiments
Flower beds prepared for winter
Forest conservation
Furniture, bedroom, made of orange crates

---

[1] Compiled from replies to NYA Circular Y-45.

APPENDIX D

Gardening
Golf course rehabilitated (put in sandtraps and hazards, resurfaced tees)
Golf course, shelters made
Grandstand roof dismantled
Grass planted
Grounds beautified
Grounds cleaned around completed construction projects (sewers)
Guide service, at historical sites
Handicraft work
Historical survey of early northern Wisconsin
Home hygiene, household management, and domestic science
Iron work, ornamental
Janitor work
Kindergarten supervision
Lagoon banks cleaned
Land cleared
Land graded
Landscaping
Laundering
Library:
    Clipping service
    Indexing
    Service
    Study hour assistance
    Traveling service
Magazines renovated
Maps:
    Copied
    Information recorded in basic township
    Made
Masonry
Murals painted
Musical instruments constructed
Music lessons
Nursery education work
Nursery work (plant)
Nursing (general)
Office work in employment work
Papering and varnishing
Parks and parkways beautified

Parks:
    Dutch oven and fireplaces constructed
    Ravines cleaned and grubbed
    Rehabilitated
Patterns, sewing, interpreted
Pavements constructed
Pillows made
Pipe laid
Plaster plaques, bookends, etc., made
Plastering
Playground:
    Construction of park area
    Equipment:
        Installed
        Made
        Manufactured
    Improvement of
Plumbing and electric fixtures installed
Posts set
Pottery
Poultry:
    Raising
    Reports kept
Pump house constructed
Poultry houses cleaned
Quilting
Recreation:
    Equipment (nets, etc.) made
    Facilities improved
    Supervision or leadership
Reporting
Research work
Retaining walls built
Roadbed, old, removed
Roads and roadways, constructed
Roads, graded
Roofing
Rugs:
    Sewed
    Rag, woven
School busses and truck repaired
School children, hot lunches prepared for and served
Seedlings and trees planted

Sewers and drains:
  Cleaned
  Constructed
Sewer mains relaid
Sewing, home
Sheetmetal work
Shelters and feed stations constructed for birds and animals
Shorthand
Shrubbery planted
Sidewalks and trails constructed
Skating pond cleaned
Skating, ice, rink, constructed
Skating rink shelter made
Soil conservation
Soil samples collected
Soil, top:
  Hauled
  Leveled
Statistics:
  Compiled and checked
  Data studied
  Surveys made
Stenographic work
Stone quarried
Street-lighting system, city, overhauled
Tables and benches constructed
Tanks (reaction) constructed
Taxidermy and craft work instruction
Terracing
Tile setting
Timber, fallen, sawed
Toys manufactured
Treatment pool dug
Trees and shrubs pruned
Trees, diseased, treated
Trucks constructed
Typing and copying
Visual aid material made (posters, scrapbooks, etc.)
Walks constructed
Weaving
Windows and doors installed
Wiring for electricity
Woodcraft
Woodcraft shop supervised in home for boys

INDEX

Ability of students, 32.
Accident compensation, 8.
Accreditation of educational institutions, 46–47.
Administration (*see also* Supervision):
    college and graduate aid program, 45.
    school aid program, 42.
Administrative:
    expenditures, 17.
    organization, 8–12, 19.
    overhead, 18, 20.
    personnel, 12–15.
    policies, Federal, 90–91.
    relations with other agencies, 19, 45, 63.
Admission requirements, higher institutions, 31.
Adult education, 85.
Adult workers, 70, 87.
Advisory committees, 9, 10, 11–12, 19, 75, 90.
Age limits for:
    student aid, 23, 77.
    vocational placement and guidance, 79.
    work projects, 48, 54, 77.
Age of:
    applicants for vocational guidance and placement, 81.
    State administrative personnel, 13.
    State directors of student aid, 14.
    student aid recipients, 35, 36.
    work projects supervisors, 14.
Agricultural:
    demonstration projects, 62, 63.
    Extension Service, 64.
    training projects, resident, 50, 51, 62, 63, 65–66, 73, 76–77, 84.
Agriculture, United States Department of, 65.
Alabama, 33, 73, 95, 96, 97, 98, 99.
Alaska, 96.
Allotments. *See* Funds.
Antisocial behavior, 6.
Applications for:
    establishment of work projects, 49.
    school aid, 24, 43.
    student aid, 31–32, 96.
    vocational placement and guidance, 81.

INDEX

Appointments. *See* Selection.
Apprentice training:
    committees, 81.
    Federal Committee on, 82.
    program, 7, 19, 79, 82.
Appropriation Acts, Federal Emergency Relief, 16.
Arizona, 95, 96, 97, 98, 99.
Arkansas, 33, 66, 73, 95, 96, 97, 98, 99.
Atlanta, Georgia, 40.
Attendance, 5, 43, 48, 74, 86.
Blind, schools for, 40.
Bricklaying classes, 73.
Building projects, 40–41, 50, 61, 62, 63, 68–69. *See also* Construction projects.
Bureau of Immigration and Naturalization, New York City, 65.
California, 54, 55, 56, 95, 96, 97, 98, 99.
Census of unemployment, 86.
Certification:
    agencies, 10.
    student aid, 46.
    work projects, 8, 48.
Chief State school officer, 23, 24, 26, 46.
Child labor, 48.
Civilian Conservation Corps, 6, 53, 81, 84.
Civil service employees, 65.
Clerical projects, 41, 51, 61, 62, 63, 65.
College aid. *See* Student aid.
College and graduate aid. *See* Student aid.
Colleges:
    attended by recipients of student aid, 37–38.
    educational standards, 46.
    eligible for student aid, 23.
    enrollments, 9, 31, 88.
    financial aid to students, 5, 26, 28, 44, 95.
    number participating in student aid, 30.
    relationships with NYA, 45.
    work plans, 27.
Colorado, 95, 96, 97, 98, 99.
Committee:
    on Apprentice Training, 82.
    Coordinating, WPA, 50.
Committees. *See* Advisory committees.
Community:
    projects, 40, 50.
    size and duration of work projects, 60.
Connecticut, 39, 72–80, 95, 96, 97, 98, 99.
Connecticut College for Women, 39.

Conservation projects, 50, 62, 63.
Construction projects, 42, 58, 62, 68–70. *See also* Building projects.
Continuation schooling, 4, 71, 78.
Control:
    decentralized, 20, 21, 63, 90.
    institutions of higher learning, 46.
Cooperation with other agencies, 11, 12, 18, 20, 77, 81, 90, 91.
Cornell University Medical College, 41.
Cosponsors, 10, 12, 18, 49, 63, 64, 67, 73, 76, 77, 100–101.
Cost:
    student aid program, 28.
    vocational guidance program, 81.
    women's camps, 84.
    work projects program, 77, 84.
    work training for out-of-school youth, 78.
Counseling. *See* Guidance.
County agencies as sponsors, 63.
Curriculum, 5, 41, 78, 88.
Decatur, Illinois, 72.
Delaware, 95, 96, 97, 98, 99.
Delinquency, 38, 40, 76.
Demonstration projects, agricultural, 62, 63.
Department:
    of Agriculture, United States, 65.
    of Labor, United States, 17, 19, 79, 82.
    of the Treasury, United States, 9.
Depression, effects of, 2, 4, 5, 89.
Deputy executive director, 9, 10, 12.
District of Columbia, 9, 33, 81, 95, 96, 97, 98, 99.
District supervisors, 10, 11, 50.
Division of Education Projects, FERA, 82–83.
Divisions:
    of N Y A, 10, 80.
    of W P A, 10, 49, 62, 69–70, 74.
Duration:
    of employment on work projects, 58, 59, 60, 61.
    of work projects program, 77.
Earnings:
    student aid, 25, 27, 31.
    work projects, 49, 53, 99.
Education:
    and income, 5, 44.
    and work experience combined, 78, 88.
    applicants for vocational guidance and placement, 81.
    as a problem of youth, 1.
    continuation of, 89.
    emergency classes, 72.
    facilitation of, 70.

Education—Continued.
    of out-of-school youth, 4–5, 43, 70, 72.
    projects, 42, 62.
    Projects Division, FERA, 82–83.
    State administrative personnel, 13.
    State directors of student aid, 14.
    work projects supervisors, 14.
    youth on work projects, 54, 55.
Educational:
    achievement, recipients of student aid, 32, 34.
    agencies, 70, 71.
    camps for women, 7, 17, 19, 51, 79, 82–85.
    concepts and policies, 88–89.
    contributions of NYA, 21.
    experience of youth on work projects, 71.
    experimentation, 88.
    facilities, 4–5.
    maintenance, 43–44, 77, 88.
    motives in relief, 6.
    needs of youth, 5.
    objectives, 88.
    opportunities, 3, 4, 5, 88.
    provision for youth on work projects, 70–75.
    qualifications of national administrative personnel, 12.
    qualifications of youth on work projects, 78.
    standards of institutions, 46.
    value of college and graduate aid programs, 46.
    values of work projects, 69–70, 77.
Eligibility:
    for student aid, 23, 24, 26, 87.
    of institutions for student aid, 46.
    of Negro graduate students, 27.
Emergency:
    agencies, 58.
    education classes, 72.
Employment (see also Placement):
    and placement statistics, 4.
    and Safety, Division of WPA, 10.
    and work experience, 55.
    as factor in work projects, 78.
    characteristics of families of student aid recipients, 35–36.
    duration on work projects, 58, 59, 60, 61.
    of youth leaving work projects, 56, 57, 58.
    offices, 49.
    on work projects, 52.
    Service, United States, 10, 49, 79, 80.
    State services, 10, 79.
    statistics, 4.

Engineering survey of construction projects, 69–70.
Enrollments:
  college, 9.
  graduate, 31.
  public school, 31.
  school and college, 88.
  student aid, 29, 30, 31.
  undergraduate, 31.
  women's camps, 83.
Evaluation:
  construction projects, 69–70.
  of NYA program, 86–91.
  of student aid program, 42–47.
  of work projects program, 76–78.
Executive committee, NYA, 9, 10.
Executive director, 9, 10.
Executive Order:
  No. 6750–C, 82.
  No. 7086, 7, 8, 92–93.
  No. 7164, 93–94.
Expenditures (*see also* Funds):
  administrative, 17.
  for national office, 17.
  for school aid, 6–7, 42.
  for State administrative offices, 17.
  for student aid, 28.
  for student aid by institutions of higher learning, 44.
  for vocational guidance programs, 81.
  for wages, 49.
  for women's camps, 17.
  for work projects, 17, 51.
  per youth, 18, 20.
  per youth on student aid, 18.
  per youth on work projects, 18, 51, 53.
  total, 17, 20.
Experimentation, 21–22, 76–77, 88, 89.
Extension Service, Agricultural, 64.
Families:
  financial ability, 43.
  of college and graduate aid recipients, 35, 36.
  relief, 76.
  size of, youth on work projects, 54.
Federal:
  aid, 44, 46.
  Committee on Apprentice Training, 82.
  Emergency Relief Administration, 6, 23, 82–83.
  Emergency Relief Appropriation Acts, 16.

Fellowships, 28, 95.
Finance:
    Division of NYA, 10.
    Division of WPA, 10.
Financial:
    ability of parents, 43.
    assistance to college and graduate students, 95.
    assistance to students provided by institutions, 5, 26, 28, 44, 95.
Florida, 33, 95, 96, 97, 98, 99.
Foremen, 71, 72, 74, 90.
Forest preservation, 64.
Funds (*see also* Expenditures):
    for apprentice training, 82.
    for student aid, 24–25, 26, 28, 31, 37, 38, 44–45.
    for women's camps, 83.
    for work projects, 51–76.
    reduction, 15.
    source, 9.
Georgia, 33, 40, 72, 95, 96, 97, 98, 99.
Grants-in-aid, 26, 28, 95.
Ground and building maintenance projects, 40–41.
Guidance, 2, 4, 5, 10, 11, 19, 78, 79–82, 83, 84, 87, 88, 89.
Guidance and Placement, Division of NYA, 10.
Hawaii, 96.
Health:
    agencies, 81.
    classes, 40.
    education, 83.
    of youth aided, 70, 89.
Highway projects, 50, 62, 63, 64.
Home economics, 40, 42, 51, 61, 62, 63, 65, 66, 72, 73, 83.
Hot Spring County, Arkansas, 66.
Hours of work, 25, 27, 49.
Hours worked on work projects, 52, 99.
Idaho, 95, 96, 97, 98, 99.
Illinois, 72, 95, 96, 97, 98, 99.
Immigration and Naturalization, Bureau of New York City, 65.
Income, 5, 35, 36, 44, 76.
Indiana, 72, 80, 95, 96, 97, 98, 99.
Industry, private, 49, 56, 57, 58, 78, 81–82, 87, 89.
Iowa, 95, 96, 97, 98, 99.
Job:
    blind-alley, 4.
    preference, 3.
    specialization, 1.
Joeckel, Carleton B., 68.
Junior colleges, 37, 38.

INDEX 111

Junior Placement Service, 7, 79, 80, 81.
Kansas, 54, 55, 64, 95, 96, 97, 98, 99.
Kentucky, 33, 54, 55, 56, 67, 72, 80, 95, 96, 97, 98, 99.
Labor:
    markets, 87.
    supply, 45.
    United States Department of, 17, 19, 79, 82.
Leadership, 50, 51, 61, 62, 63, 89, 90.
Leisure time, 3, 81.
Library projects, 40, 41, 51, 61, 62, 63, 67–68.
Lincoln, Nebraska, 40.
Loans to students, 26, 28, 95.
Local government, 44, 63, 76.
Louisiana, 54, 95, 96, 97, 98, 99.
Lucas County, Ohio, 73.
Maine, 67, 95, 96, 97, 98, 99.
Maintenance of school youth, 5, 43, 77, 88.
Maryland, 67, 95, 96, 97, 98, 99.
Massachusetts, 67, 80, 95, 96, 97, 98, 99.
Michigan, 54, 55, 56, 62, 95, 96, 97, 98, 99.
Migration of college aid students, 33.
Minnesota, 54, 55, 56, 95, 96, 97, 98, 99.
Minority groups, 25, 33.
Mississippi, 33, 73, 95, 96, 97, 98, 99.
Missouri, 33, 64, 95, 96, 97, 98, 99.
Montana, 67, 95, 96, 97, 98, 99.
Morale of youth, 89.
Morgan County, Kentucky, 67.
Museum work projects, 51, 61, 62, 63.
National:
    Industrial Recovery Act, 82.
    Youth Service Administration, 22.
Nebraska, 40, 54, 55, 67, 95, 96, 97, 98, 99.
Negro:
    administrative personnel, 12, 13.
    Affairs, Division of, NYA, 10.
    girls, 73.
    graduate aid, 27.
    school for blind, 40.
    student aid, 33–34, 35, 36.
    work projects program, 54.
    youth, 54.
Nevada, 95, 96, 97, 98, 99.
New Hampshire, 54, 55, 95, 96, 97, 98, 99.
New Jersey, 67, 95, 96, 97, 98, 99.
New Mexico, 67, 73, 95, 96, 97, 98, 99.
New York City, 9, 41, 54, 55, 65, 95, 96, 97, 98, 99.
New York State, 95, 96, 97, 98, 99.

North Carolina, 33, 67, 80, 95, 96, 97, 98, 99.
North Dakota, 64, 95, 96, 97, 98, 99.
Nursery school projects, 51, 62, 63.
Occupational:
    characteristics of youth on work projects, 55.
    classes, 80.
    surveys, 38.
    training, 71.
Occupations, parents of student aid recipients, 35, 36.
Ohio, 54, 55, 56, 73, 74, 95, 96, 97, 98, 99.
Oklahoma, 64, 68, 95, 96, 97, 98, 99.
Oregon, 95, 96, 97, 98, 99.
Organization, 8–12.
Out-of-school youth, 3, 4–5, 6, 21, 43, 51, 70–72, 76, 78. *See also* Youth.
Passamaquoddy Village, Maine, 75. *See also* Quoddy training projects.
Pennsylvania, 95, 96, 97, 98, 99.
Personnel:
    administrative, 12–15, 19.
    characteristics, 14–15, 21.
    national office, 9.
    qualifications, 22.
    records of youth receiving guidance, 80.
    replacement, 14, 20.
    selection, 14, 15, 19.
    State and district, 11.
    turn-over, 14, 20.
Placement, 4, 79–82, 89. *See also* Employment.
Prairie View State Normal and Industrial College for Negroes, Texas, 73.
President of the United States, The, 9, 10.
Private schools, 37, 38, 46.
Public schools, 24, 31, 37, 38, 46.
Public service projects, 50.
Puerto Rico, 95.
Quoddy training projects, 75, 77.
Quotas:
    student aid, 24–25, 26–27, 31, 32, 33, 37, 38, 96.
    work projects, 48, 75.
Recipients of student aid, 15, 16, 23, 29–36, 42, 43, 46, 97.
Recreation:
    activities, 40, 83.
    areas, 64.
    facilities, construction, 68.
    group, 83.
    leadership, 50, 51, 61, 62, 63.
    opportunities, 80.
    projects, 42.
Regional directors, 10, 12.

INDEX

Rehabilitation of youth, 5–6.
Relief:
    among families of recipients, 35, 36.
    Appropriations Acts, 16.
    as a criterion for employment, 87.
    families, 76.
    functions, 8.
    groups, 43.
    objectives, 88.
    problem, the, 86–87.
    quotas on work project programs, 48.
    status of youth employed on work projects, 52.
    wages, 84.
    work projects, 81.
    youth, 59.
Reorganization of school districts, 43.
Reports and Records, Division of, NYA, 10.
Research:
    and statistical services, 8.
    and Statistics, Division of, NYA, 10.
    projects, 38–39, 50, 62, 63.
Resident agricultural training projects, 50, 51, 62, 63, 65–66, 73, 76–77, 84.
Rhode Island, 95, 96, 97, 98, 99.
Roads. *See* Highway projects.
Rural:
    areas, 67.
    county quotas, 32, 33.
    development projects, 50.
    residence of work projects youth, 61.
Russell, John Dale, 82.
Safety:
    conditions, 70.
    regulations, 8.
Salaries, 13, 14.
Scholarships, 5, 26, 28, 44, 95.
School aid. *See* Student aid.
School lunch projects, 51, 62, 63.
Secondary schools, 5, 25, 30, 42, 88. *See also* Student aid.
Selection:
    and assignment of youth, 8.
    of staff, 14, 15, 19.
    of students, 23, 24, 31–32, 42, 45.
Sewing projects, 51, 61, 62, 63.
Sex:
    administrative personnel, 12, 13, 14.
    recipients of student aid, 31, 34, 35, 36.
    work projects, youth, 52, 53–54, 56.

Shawnee, Oklahoma, 68.
Soil conservation, 38, 64.
South Carolina, 33, 95, 96, 97, 98, 99.
South Dakota, 64, 95, 96, 97, 98, 99.
Southeast, 98.
Southern States, 33, 64.
Southwest, 98.
Sponsors. *See* Cosponsors.
State:
    Agricultural and Mechanical Institute, Alabama, 73.
    cooperation, 22.
    departments as sponsors, 63.
    directors, 9, 10, 11, 13, 14, 23, 24, 26, 46, 49, 50, 71, 72, 74, 83, 84.
    education departments, 72.
    employment services, 10, 79.
    organization, 10, 11.
    responsibility for education, 43–44.
    supervisors, 11, 13.
    WPA director, 49.
Statistical:
    projects, 40, 50, 51, 61, 63.
    reporting, 8.
    Review Section, WPA, 50.
Student aid. *See also* Secondary schools:
    age limits, 23, 77.
    applications, 31–32, 96.
    characteristics of recipients, 33–36.
    college and graduate aid, 9, 25–28, 31, 38–42, 44–47.
    communities aided, 32.
    eligibility, 81, 87.
    enrollments, 29, 30, 31.
    establishment, 23.
    evaluation, 42–47.
    Executive Order No. 7164, 93.
    expenditures, 17, 18, 20, 28–29.
    from institutions, 28, 44.
    fund allocations, 37–38.
    institutions participating, 30, 37–38.
    mobility of students, 33.
    program, 6, 7, 9, 10, 16, 19, 23–47, 77.
    projects, 38–42.
    quotas, 31–32, 37–38, 96.
    scholastic achievement of recipients, 32.
    school aid, 6–7, 23–25, 31, 32, 33, 34–36, 42–44, 77, 96.
    State directors, 14.
    State resources, 44.
    supervision, 10, 11.
    wages, 31.

Superintendents of public schools, 24.
Supervision, 10, 42–43, 46, 77, 78. *See also* Administration.
Supervisors, 10, 11, 13, 14. 50, 80, 90.
Supplies, 9.
Teachers colleges, 37, 38.
Technical schools, 37, 38.
Tenant farmers, 65.
Tennessee, 33, 95, 96, 97, 98, 99.
Texas, 33, 64, 80, 95, 96, 97, 98, 99.
Texas Youth Administration, 73.
Textbooks, 43.
Trade school:
    as cosponsor, 73.
    courses, 72.
Training:
    job, 87.
    occupational, 71.
    on work projects, 71, 74.
    opportunities, 80.
    out-of-school youth, 78.
    resident agricultural projects, 50, 51, 62, 63, 65–66, 73, 76–77, 84.
    vocational, 6, 54, 55, 81.
Transportation:
    of pupils, 43
    to women's camps, 84.
Treasury, United States, Department of the, 9.
Tuition costs, 5, 65.
Turn-over:
    of personnel, 14, 20.
    of youth on work projects, 56–58.
Underprivileged youth, 88.
Unemployed women. *See* Women's camps.
Unemployed youth, 5, 48, 53, 70, 79, 89.
Unemployment census, 86.
Union College, Lincoln, Nebraska, 40.
Universities:
    educational standards, 46.
    eligible for student aid, 23.
    enrollments, 31.
    expenditures for student aid, 44.
    participating in student aid, 26, 30, 37–38.
    relationships with NYA, 45.
    work plans, 27.
University of Alabama, 73.
University of Minnesota, 6.
Upstream Engineering Conference, 1936, 63.
Utah, 95, 96, 97, 98, 99.

Vermont, 95, 96, 97, 98, 99.
Virginia, 33, 95, 96, 97, 98, 99.
Vocational:
    classes, 72, 73 (trade).
    counselors. *See* Guidance.
    education, 70.
    guidance. *See* Guidance.
    placement. *See* Placement.
    schools, 74.
    training. *See* Training.
Wages, 4, 25, 27, 31, 49, 52–53, 58, 59, 77, 84, 87.
Washington, 73, 95, 96, 97, 98, 99.
Wayne County, Kentucky, 67.
West Virginia, 54, 55, 56, 95, 96, 97, 98, 99.
Wetumka, Oklahoma, 68.
Wisconsin, 80, 95, 96, 97, 98, 99.
Women's camps, 7, 17, 19, 51, 79, 82–85.
Work experience, 13, 14, 55, 76, 78, 81, 88, 89.
Work projects:
    age limits, 48, 54, 77.
    application to establish, 49.
    approval, 11, 49–50.
    assignment and classification of youth, 48.
    benefit to local communities, 76, 78, 90.
    certification of eligible youth, 8.
    characteristics of youth, 52, 54–56.
    classification, 50–51.
    cost per enrollee, 84.
    definition, 19.
    Division, 10.
    duration of employment, 58–61.
    earnings, 53, 99.
    educational provisions, 70–75.
    evaluation, 50, 69–70, 76–78.
    expenditures, 17, 18, 20, 51, 53.
    funds, 9.
    hours of work, 49.
    hours worked, 99.
    objectives, 7.
    planning, 11.
    relief projects, 81.
    relief status of youth, 48, 52, 87.
    residence of youth, 61.
    safety regulations, 8.
    sponsors, 49.
    supervisors, 13, 14, 50.
    turn-over, 56–58.

Work projects—Continued.
    types of projects, 61–70, 102–104.
    wages, 49, 52–53, 87.
    youth employed, 52–61, 87.
Workers' education, 84.
Works Progress Administration, 7, 8, 9, 10, 11, 17, 18, 18–19, 20, 24, 36, 48, 49, 50, 51, 58, 62, 69–70, 72, 73, 74.
Workshop projects, 51, 62, 63, 66–67.
Wyoming, 95, 96, 97, 98, 99.
Youth (*see also* Out-of-school youth):
    definition, 1.
    problem, 1–7.
    Service Administration, 22.
    urgent problems, 89–90.

RESEARCH STAFF AND CONSULTANTS

This list gives the names of the various consultants and members of the research staff of the Advisory Committee on Education. The names starred are those of major consultants of the Committee, of members of the staff who were responsible for the supervision of major staff units, and of authors of studies published by the Committee.

FLOYD W. REEVES, *Director of Studies*
PAUL T. DAVID, *Assistant Director of Studies*
LAVERNE BURCHFIELD, *Editor*

Alexander, Fred M.
Alves, Henry F.
Asserson, Grace P.
Baer, Joseph A.
Bagley, William C.
Bahr, Clarence L.
*Bair, Frederick H.
Barrett, Edwin J.
Benjamin, Hazel C.
*Bentley, Jerome H.
Blander, Margaret M.
*Blauch, Lloyd E.
*Bradford, Minnie B.
Bridgman, Ralph P.
*Broach, Howell H.
*Brown, Clara M.
Butler, Clare W.
*Campbell, Doak S.
Carpenter, O. F.
*Cocking, Walter D.
*Cooper, Thomas P.
Cornell, Francis G.
Coyle, David Cushman
*Crawford, Finla G.
Daoust, Joseph H.
*Davis, Anne
Dickerman, Watson B.
DuBois, Marion
*Edwards, Newton
Elicker, Paul E.

Emerson, Lynn A.
Exton, Elaine
Fairbanks, Mary H.
Foster, Jeannette H.
*Frederic, Katherine A.
Gerberich, Joseph R.
*Gilmore, Charles H.
Gold, Norman L.
Grace, Alonzo G.
Groves, Harold M.
*Hamilton, Robert R.
Harrison, Mary Roberts
*Harvey, Oswald L.
Hausrath, Alfred H.
*Heer, Clarence
*Holland, Kenneth
Houle, Cyril O.
*Hughes, Raymond M.
Irby, Nolen M.
*Iversen, William L.
*Joeckel, Carleton B.
*Johnson, Palmer O.
*Jordan, Floyd
*Judd, Charles H.
Kauffman, Roma Kaye
Koos, Leonard V.
*Lancelot, William H.
Lane, Jessie A.
*Lawler, Eugene S.
Lee, Charles A.

Lippitt, Marian B.
Little, Harry A.
Loebl, Stephen M.
Mac Auley, Mary V.
*Morgan, Barton
Morphet, Edgar L.
*Mort, Paul R.
Mosier, Earl E.
Neblett, Thomas F.
*Newcomer, Mabel
Norton, Thomas L.
Olson, Marion E.
*Parker, Julia O'Connor
Peck, Charles R.
Peterson, Elmer T.
Pope, Eugenia
*Power, Leonard
*Powers, J. Orin
*Ramsey, Fredlyn
Reid, Charles F.

Rhodes, Opal T.
*Richey, Herman G.
*Russell, John Dale
Rybczynski, Henrietta M.
Schrader, Carl L.
Skinner, Mary E.
*Smith, C. Currien
*Smith, Lewis W.
*Smith, Payson
Studenski, Paul
Tanruther, Edgar M.
Tingley, Helen
Tyler, Tracy F.
*Weaver, Robert C.
West, Roscoe L.
*Wilkerson, Doxey A.
Williams, Kenneth R.
*Works, George A.
*Wright, Frank W.

CHILDREN AND YOUTH
Social Problems and Social Policy

An Arno Press Collection

Abt, Henry Edward. **The Care, Cure and Education of the Crippled Child.** 1924

Addams, Jane. **My Friend, Julia Lathrop.** 1935

American Academy of Pediatrics. **Child Health Services and Pediatric Education:** Report of the Committee for the Study of Child Health Services. 1949

American Association for the Study and Prevention of Infant Mortality. **Transactions of the First Annual Meeting of the American Association for the Study and Prevention of Infant Mortality.** 1910

Baker, S. Josephine. **Fighting For Life.** 1939

Bell, Howard M. **Youth Tell Their Story:** A Study of the Conditions and Attitudes of Young People in Maryland Between the Ages of 16 and 24. 1938

Bossard, James H. S. and Eleanor S. Boll, editors. **Adolescents in Wartime.** 1944

Bossard, James H. S., editor. **Children in a Depression Decade.** 1940

Brunner, Edmund DeS. **Working With Rural Youth.** 1942

Care of Dependent Children in the Late Nineteenth and Early Twentieth Centuries. Introduction by Robert H. Bremner. 1974

Care of Handicapped Children. Introduction by Robert H. Bremner. 1974

[Chenery, William L. and Ella A. Merritt, editors]. **Standards of Child Welfare:** A Report of the Children's Bureau Conferences, May and June, 1919. 1919

The Child Labor Bulletin, 1912, 1913. 1974

Children In Confinement. Introduction by Robert M. Mennel. 1974

Children's Bureau Studies. Introduction by William M. Schmidt. 1974

Clopper, Edward N. **Child Labor in City Streets.** 1912

David, Paul T. **Barriers To Youth Employment.** 1942

Deutsch, Albert. **Our Rejected Children.** 1950

Drucker, Saul and Maurice Beck Hexter. **Children Astray.** 1923

Duffus, R[obert] L[uther] and L. Emmett Holt, Jr. **L. Emmett Holt: Pioneer of a Children's Century.** 1940

Fuller, Raymond G. **Child Labor and the Constitution.** 1923

Holland, Kenneth and Frank Ernest Hill. **Youth in the CCC.** 1942

Jacoby, George Paul. **Catholic Child Care in Nineteenth Century New York:** With a Correlated Summary of Public and Protestant Child Welfare. 1941

Johnson, Palmer O. and Oswald L. Harvey. **The National Youth Administration.** 1938

The Juvenile Court. Introduction by Robert M. Mennel. 1974

Klein, Earl E. **Work Accidents to Minors in Illinois.** 1938

Lane, Francis E. **American Charities and the Child of the Immigrant:** A Study of Typical Child Caring Institutions in New York and Massachusetts Between the Years 1845 and 1880. 1932

The Legal Rights of Children. Introduction by Sanford N. Katz. 1974

Letchworth, William P[ryor]. **Homes of Homeless Children:** A Report on Orphan Asylums and Other Institutions for the Care of Children. [1903]

Lorwin, Lewis. **Youth Work Programs:** Problems and Policies. 1941

Lundberg, Emma O[ctavia] and Katharine F. Lenroot. **Illegitimacy As A Child-Welfare Problem, Parts 1 and 2.** 1920/1921

New York State Commission on Relief for Widowed Mothers. **Report of the New York State Commission on Relief for Widowed Mothers.** 1914

Otey, Elizabeth Lewis. **The Beginnings of Child Labor Legislation in Certain States;** A Comparative Study. 1910

Phillips, Wilbur C. **Adventuring For Democracy.** 1940

Polier, Justine Wise. **Everyone's Children, Nobody's Child:** A Judge Looks At Underprivileged Children in the United States. 1941

Proceedings of the Annual Meeting of the National Child Labor Committee, 1905, 1906. 1974

Rainey, Homer P. **How Fare American Youth?** 1940

Reeder, Rudolph R. **How Two Hundred Children Live and Learn.** 1910

Security and Services For Children. 1974

Sinai, Nathan and Odin W. Anderson. **EMIC (Emergency Maternity and Infant Care):** A Study of Administrative Experience. 1948

Slingerland, W. H. **Child-Placing in Families:** A Manual For Students and Social Workers. 1919

[Solenberger], Edith Reeves. **Care and Education of Crippled Children in the United States.** 1914

Spencer, Anna Garlin and Charles Wesley Birtwell, editors. **The Care of Dependent, Neglected and Wayward Children:** Being a Report of the Second Section of the International Congress of Charities, Correction and Philanthropy, Chicago, June, 1893. 1894

Theis, Sophie Van Senden. **How Foster Children Turn Out.** 1924

Thurston, Henry W. **The Dependent Child:** A Story of Changing Aims and Methods in the Care of Dependent Children. 1930

U.S. Advisory Committee on Education. **Report of the Committee, February, 1938.** 1938

The United States Children's Bureau, 1912-1972. 1974

White House Conference on Child Health and Protection.
Dependent and Neglected Children: Report of the Committee on Socially Handicapped — Dependency and Neglect. 1933

White House Conference on Child Health and Protection.
Organization for the Care of Handicapped Children, National, State, Local. 1932

White House Conference on Children in a Democracy. **Final Report of the White House Conference on Children in A Democracy.** [1942]

Wilson, Otto. **Fifty Years' Work With Girls, 1883-1933:** A Story of the Florence Crittenton Homes. 1933

Wrenn, C. Gilbert and D. L. Harley. **Time On Their Hands:** A Report on Leisure, Recreation, and Young People. 1941